MznLnx

Missing Links Exam Preps

Exam Prep for

Essentials of Entrepreneurship and Small Business Management

Zimmerer & Scarborough, 5th Edition

The MznLnx Exam Prep is your link from the texbook and lecture to your exams.
The MznLnx Exam Preps are unauthorized and comprehensive reviews of your textbooks.

All material provided by MznLnx and Rico Publications (c) 2010
Textbook publishers and textbook authors do not particpate in or contribute to these reviews.

MznLnx

Rico Publications

Exam Prep for Essentials of Entrepreneurship and Small Business Management
5th Edition
Zimmerer & Scarborough

Publisher: Raymond Houge
Assistant Editor: Michael Rouger
Text and Cover Designer: Lisa Buckner
Marketing Manager: Sara Swagger
Project Manager, Editorial Production: Jerry Emerson
Art Director: Vernon Lowerui

Product Manager: Dave Mason
Editorial Assitant: Rachel Guzmanji
Pedagogy: Debra Long
Cover Image: Jim Reed/Getty Images
Text and Cover Printer: City Printing, Inc.
Compositor: Media Mix, Inc.

(c) 2010 Rico Publications
ALL RIGHTS RESERVED. No part of this work
covered by the copyright may be reproduced or
used in any form or by an means--graphic, electronic,
or mechanical, including photocopying, recording,
taping, Web distribution, information storage, and
retrieval systems, or in any other manner--without the
written permission of the publisher.

Printed in the United States
ISBN:

For more information about our products, contact us at:
Dave.Mason@RicoPublications.com

For permission to use material from this text or
product, submit a request online to:
Dave.Mason@RicoPublications.com

Contents

CHAPTER 1
The Foundations of Entrepreneurship — 1

CHAPTER 2
Inside the Entrepreneurial Mind: From Ideas to Reality — 12

CHAPTER 3
Designing a Competitive Business Model and Building a Solid Strategic Plan — 17

CHAPTER 4
Conducting a Feasibility Analysis and Crafting a Winning Business Plan — 24

CHAPTER 5
Forms of Business Ownership — 31

CHAPTER 6
Franchising and the Entrepreneur — 38

CHAPTER 7
Buying an Existing Business — 45

CHAPTER 8
Building a Powerful Marketing Plan — 55

CHAPTER 9
E-Commerce and the Entrepreneur — 65

CHAPTER 10
Pricing Strategies — 74

CHAPTER 11
Creating a Successful Financial Plan — 78

CHAPTER 12
Managing Cash Flow — 87

CHAPTER 13
Sources of Financing: Debt and Equity — 92

CHAPTER 14
Choosing the Right Location and Layout — 101

CHAPTER 15
Global Aspects of Entrepreneurship — 108

CHAPTER 16
Building a New Venture Team and Planning for the Next Generation — 115

ANSWER KEY — 127

TO THE STUDENT

COMPREHENSIVE

The *MznLnx* Exam Prep series is designed to help you pass your exams. Editors at MznLnx review your textbooks and then prepare these practice exams to help you master the textbook material. Unlike study guides, workbooks, and practice tests provided by the texbook publisher and textbook authors, *MznLnx* gives you **all** of the material in each chapter in exam form, not just samples, so you can be sure to nail your exam.

MECHANICAL

The MznLnx Exam Prep series creates exams that will help you learn the subject matter as well as test you on your understanding. Each question is designed to help you master the concept. Just working through the exams, you gain an understanding of the subject--its a simple mechanical process that produces success.

INTEGRATED STUDY GUIDE AND REVIEW

MznLnx is not just a set of exams designed to test you, its also a comprehensive review of the subject content. Each exam question is also a review of the concept, making sure that you will get the answer correct without having to go to other sources of material. You learn as you go! Its the easiest way to pass an exam.

HUMOR

Studying can be tedious and dry. MznLnx's instructional design includes moderate humor within the exam questions on occassion, to break the tedium and revitalize the brain

Chapter 1. The Foundations of Entrepreneurship   1

1. _____ according to Onuoha (2007) is the practice of starting new organizations or revitalizing mature organizations, particularly new businesses generally in response to identified opportunities. _____ is often a difficult undertaking, as a vast majority of new businesses fail. Entrepreneurial activities are substantially different depending on the type of organization that is being started.
   a. Entrepreneurship
   b. A Stake in the Outcome
   c. AAAI
   d. A4e

2. _____, commonly abbreviated to Gen X, is a term used to refer to a generational cohort of children born after the baby boom ended and usually prior to the 1980s

   The term _____ has been used in demography, the social sciences, and marketing, though it is most often used in popular culture.

   In the U.S. _____ was originally referred to as the 'baby bust' generation because of the drop in the birth rate following the baby boom.

   a. Adam Smith
   b. Affiliation
   c. Abraham Harold Maslow
   d. Generation X

3. _____ is a term used to describe the demographic cohort following Generation X. Its members are often referred to as 'Millennials' or 'Echo Boomers') . There are no precise dates for when Gen Y begins and ends. Most commentators use dates from the early 1980s to early 1990s.
   a. Benjamin R. Barber
   b. Giovanni Agnelli
   c. Generation Y
   d. David Wittig

4. _____ is the probability that an individual will keep his or her job; a job with a high level of _____ is such that a person with the job would have a small chance of becoming unemployed.

   _____ is dependent on economy, prevailing business conditions, and the individual's personal skills. It has been found that people have more _____ in times of economic expansion and less in times of a recession.

   a. Just cause
   b. Job security
   c. Multiple careers
   d. Hygiene factors

5. _____ is the temporary suspension or permanent termination of employment of an employee or (more commonly) a group of employees for business reasons, such as the decision that certain positions are no longer necessary or a business slow-down or interruption in work. Originally the term '_____' referred exclusively to a temporary interruption in work, as when factory work cyclically falls off. However, in recent times the term can also refer to the permanent elimination of a position.
   a. Retirement
   b. Termination of employment
   c. Wrongful dismissal
   d. Layoff

6. A _____ is a professional who provides advice in a particular area of expertise such as management, accountancy, the environment, entertainment, technology, law , human resources, marketing, medicine, finance, economics, public affairs, communication, engineering, sound system design, graphic design, or waste management.

A _____ is usually an expert or a professional in a specific field and has a wide knowledge of the subject matter. A _____ usually works for a consultancy firm or is self-employed, and engages with multiple and changing clients.

a. Consultant
c. 28-hour day
b. 1990 Clean Air Act
d. 33 Strategies of War

7. An _____ is a person who has possession of an enterprise and assumes significant accountability for the inherent risks and the outcome. It is an ambitious leader who combines land, labor, and capital to create and market new goods or services. The term is a loanword from French and was first defined by the Irish economist Richard Cantillon.
   a. A Stake in the Outcome
   c. Entrepreneur
   b. AAAI
   d. A4e

8. _____ is the state or fact of exclusive rights and control over property, which may be an object, land/real estate or intellectual property. An _____ right is also referred to as title. The concept of _____ has existed for thousands of years and in all cultures.
   a. A4e
   c. Emanation of the state
   b. A Stake in the Outcome
   d. Ownership

9. In decision theory and estimation theory, the _____ of an estimator, $\hat{\theta}$, of an unknown parameter of the distribution, θ, is the expected value of the loss function

$$R(\theta, \hat{\theta}) = \mathbb{E}_\theta L(\theta, \hat{\theta}) = \int L(\theta, \hat{\theta}) \, dP_\theta.$$

Chapter 1. The Foundations of Entrepreneurship

where dP_θ is a probability measure parametrized by θ.

- For a scalar parameter θ and a quadratic loss function,

$$L(\theta, \hat{\theta}) = (\theta - \hat{\theta})^2$$

the _____ function becomes the mean squared error of the estimate,

$$R(\theta, \hat{\theta}) = E_\theta(\theta - \hat{\theta})^2$$

- In density estimation, the unknown parameter is probability density itself. The loss function is typically chosen to be a norm in an appropriate function space. For example, for L^2 norm,

$$L(f, \hat{f}) = \|f - \hat{f}\|_2^2$$

the _____ function becomes the mean integrated squared error

$$R(f, \hat{f}) = E\|f - \hat{f}\|^2$$

a. Linear model
c. Risk

b. Financial modeling
d. Risk aversion

10. _____ describes the situation when output from (or information about the result of) an event or phenomenon in the past will influence the same event/phenomenon in the present or future. When an event is part of a chain of cause-and-effect that forms a circuit or loop, then the event is said to 'feed back' into itself.

_____ is also a synonym for:

- _____ signal; the information about the initial event that is the basis for subsequent modification of the event.
- _____ loop; the causal path that leads from the initial generation of the _____ signal to the subsequent modification of the event.

_____ is a mechanism, process or signal that is looped back to control a system within itself. Such a loop is called a _____ loop.

a. Feedback loop
c. 1990 Clean Air Act

b. Feedback
d. Positive feedback

11. A _____ is a formal statement of a set of business goals, the reasons why they are believed attainable, and the plan for reaching those goals. It may also contain background information about the organization or team attempting to reach those goals.

The business goals may be defined for for-profit or for non-profit organizations.

a. Time management
b. Business plan
c. Distributed management
d. Crisis management

12. Engineering _____ is the permissible limit of variation in

1. a physical dimension,
2. a measured value or physical property of a material, manufactured object, system, or service,
3. other measured values (such as temperature, humidity, etc.)
4. in engineering and safety, a physical distance or space (_____), as in a truck (lorry), train or boat under a bridge as well as a train in a tunnel

Dimensions, properties, or conditions may vary within certain practical limits without significantly affecting functioning of equipment or a process. _____s are specified to allow reasonable leeway for imperfections and inherent variability without compromising performance.

The _____ may be specified as a factor or percentage of the nominal value, a maximum deviation from a nominal value, an explicit range of allowed values, be specified by a note or published standard with this information, or be implied by the numeric accuracy of the nominal value. _____ can be symmetrical, as in 40±0.1, or asymmetrical, such as 40+0.2/−0.1.

a. Quality assurance
b. Root cause analysis
c. Zero defects
d. Tolerance

13. The 'business case for _____', theorizes that in a global marketplace, a company that employs a diverse workforce (both men and women, people of many generations, people from ethnically and racially diverse backgrounds etc.) is better able to understand the demographics of the marketplace it serves and is thus better equipped to thrive in that marketplace than a company that has a more limited range of employee demographics.

An additional corollary suggests that a company that supports the _____ of its workforce can also improve employee satisfaction, productivity and retention.

a. Virtual team
b. Kanban
c. Trademark
d. Diversity

14. _____ is one of the managerial functions like planning, organizing, staffing and directing. It is an important function because it helps to check the errors and to take the corrective action so that deviation from standards are minimized and stated goals of the organization are achieved in desired manner. According to modern concepts, _____ is a foreseeing action whereas earlier concept of _____ was used only when errors were detected. _____ in management means setting standards, measuring actual performance and taking corrective action.

Chapter 1. The Foundations of Entrepreneurship

a. Decision tree pruning
c. Schedule of reinforcement
b. Turnover
d. Control

15. _____, also referred to simply as a 'public offering' or 'flotation,' is when a company issues common stock or shares to the public for the first time. They are often issued by smaller, younger companies seeking capital to expand, but can also be done by large privately-owned companies looking to become publicly traded.

In an _____ the issuer may obtain the assistance of an underwriting firm, which helps it determine what type of security to issue (common or preferred), best offering price and time to bring it to market.

a. Occupational Safety and Health Administration
c. Initial public offering
b. Unemployment insurance
d. Outsourcing

16. _____ is a process and a set of procedures used to estimate the economic value of an owner's interest in a business. Valuation is used by financial market participants to determine the price they are willing to pay or receive to consummate a sale of a business. In addition to estimating the selling price of a business, the same valuation tools are often used by business appraisers to resolve disputes related to estate and gift taxation, divorce litigation, allocate business purchase price among business assets, establish a formula for estimating the value of partners' ownership interest for buy-sell agreements, and many other business and legal purposes.

a. Business valuation
c. Munn v. Illinois
b. No-FEAR Act
d. Robinson-Patman Act

17. The _____ is the labour pool in employment. It is generally used to describe those working for a single company or industry, but can also apply to a geographic region like a city, country, state, etc. The term generally excludes the employers or management, and implies those involved in manual labour.

a. Division of labour
c. Work-life balance
b. Pink-collar worker
d. Workforce

18. _____ or _____ data refers to selected population characteristics as used in government, marketing or opinion research, or the _____ profiles used in such research. Note the distinction from the term 'demography' Commonly-used _____s include race, age, income, disabilities, mobility (in terms of travel time to work or number of vehicles available), educational attainment, home ownership, employment status, and even location.

a. Affiliation
c. Demographic
b. Adam Smith
d. Abraham Harold Maslow

19. The _____ or gross domestic income (GDI), a basic measure of an economy's economic performance, is the market value of all final goods and services made within the borders of a nation in a year. _____ can be defined in three ways, all of which are conceptually identical. First, it is equal to the total expenditures for all final goods and services produced within the country in a stipulated period of time (usually a 365-day year).

a. Perfect competition
c. Human capital
b. Gross domestic product
d. Productivity management

20. _____ is an advertisement in which a particular product specifically mentions a competitor by name for the express purpose of showing why the competitor is inferior to the product naming it.

This should not be confused with parody advertisements, where a fictional product is being advertised for the purpose of poking fun at the particular advertisement, nor should it be confused with the use of a coined brand name for the purpose of comparing the product without actually naming an actual competitor. ('Wikipedia tastes better and is less filling than the Encyclopedia Galactica.')

In the 1980s, during what has been referred to as the cola wars, soft-drink manufacturer Pepsi ran a series of advertisements where people, caught on hidden camera, in a blind taste test, chose Pepsi over rival Coca-Cola.

- a. 28-hour day
- b. 1990 Clean Air Act
- c. 33 Strategies of War
- d. Comparative advertising

21. _____, commonly known as e-commerce, consists of the buying and selling of products or services over electronic systems such as the Internet and other computer networks. The amount of trade conducted electronically has grown extraordinarily with widespread Internet usage. The use of commerce is conducted in this way, spurring and drawing on innovations in electronic funds transfer, supply chain management, Internet marketing, online transaction processing, electronic data interchange (EDI), inventory management systems, and automated data collection systems.
- a. Online shopping
- b. A Stake in the Outcome
- c. Electronic Commerce
- d. A4e

22. _____ consists of the mental process of thinking involved with the process of judging the merits of multiple options and selecting one of them for action. Some simple examples include deciding whether to get up in the morning or go back to sleep, or selecting a given route for a journey. More complex examples (often decisions that affect what a person thinks or their core beliefs) include choosing a lifestyle, religious affiliation, or political position.
- a. Groups decision making
- b. Trade study
- c. Championship mobilization
- d. Choice

23. _____ is the provision of service to customers before, during and after a purchase.

According to Turban et al. (2002), '_____ is a series of activities designed to enhance the level of customer satisfaction - that is, the feeling that a product or service has met the customer expectation.'

Its importance varies by product, industry and customer; defective or broken merchandise can be exchanged, often only with a receipt and within a specified time frame.

- a. 1990 Clean Air Act
- b. 28-hour day
- c. Service rate
- d. Customer service

24. In economics, the term _____ refers to situations where the advancement of a qualified person within the hierarchy of an organization is stopped at a lower level because of some form of discrimination, most commonly sexism or racism, but since the term was coined, '_____' has also come to describe the limited advancement of the deaf, blind, disabled, aged and sexual minorities. It is an unofficial, invisible barrier that prevents women and minorities from advancing in businesses.

Chapter 1. The Foundations of Entrepreneurship 7

This situation is referred to as a 'ceiling' as there is a limitation blocking upward advancement, and 'glass' (transparent) because the limitation is not immediately apparent and is normally an unwritten and unofficial policy. This invisible barrier continues to exist, even though there are no explicit obstacles keeping minorities from acquiring advanced job positions - there are no advertisements that specifically say 'no minorities hired at this establishment', nor are there any formal orders that say 'minorities are not qualified' - but they do lie beneath the surface.

a. 1990 Clean Air Act
b. 28-hour day
c. 33 Strategies of War
d. Glass ceiling

25. A _____ is a legal document relating to the formation of a company or corporation. It is a license to form a corporation issued by state government. Its precise meaning depends upon the legal system in which it is used, but the two primary meanings are:

- In the U.S.A. a _____ is usually used as an alternative description of a corporation's articles of incorporation.
- In English and Commonwealth legal systems, a _____ is usually a simple certificate issued by the relevant government registry as confirmation of the due incorporation and valid existence of the company.

In the U.S.A. the _____ or articles of incorporation form a major constituent part of the constitutional documents of the corporation.

a. Toxic Substances Control Act
b. Civil Rights Act of 1875
c. Blue sky law
d. Certificate of Incorporation

26. _____ involves having senior executives periodically review their top executives and those in the next lower level to determine several backups for each senior position. This is important because it often takes years of grooming to develop effective senior managers. There is a critical shortage in companies of middle and top leaders for the next five years.

a. Trademark
b. Risk management
c. Kanban
d. Succession planning

27. A _____ is typically described as a deliberate plan of action to guide decisions and achieve rational outcome(s.) However, the term may also be used to denote what is actually done, even though it is unplanned.

The term may apply to government, private sector organizations and groups, and individuals.

a. 33 Strategies of War
b. 1990 Clean Air Act
c. Policy
d. 28-hour day

28. In microeconomics, industrial organization is the field which describes the behavior of firms in the marketplace with regard to production, pricing, employment and other decisions. _____ in this field range from classical issues such as opportunity cost to neoclassical concepts such as factors of production.

- Production theory basics
    - production efficiency
    - factors of production
    - total, average, and marginal product curves
    - marginal productivity
    - isoquants ' isocosts
    - the marginal rate of technical substitution
- Economic rent
    - classical factor rents
    - Paretian factor rents
- Production possibility frontier
    - what products are possible given a set of resources
    - the trade-off between producing one product rather than another
    - the marginal rate of transformation
- Production function
    - inputs
    - diminishing returns to inputs
    - the stages of production
    - shifts in a production function
- Cost theory
    - the different types of costs
        - opportunity cost
        - accounting cost or historical costs
        - transaction cost
        - sunk cost
        - marginal cost
    - the isocost line
- Cost-of-production theory of value
- Long-run cost and production functions
    - long-run average cost
    - long-run production function and efficiency
    - returns to scale and isoclines
    - minimum efficient scale
    - plant capacity
- Economies of density
- Economies of scale
    - the efficiency consequences of increasing or decreasing the level of production
- Economies of scope
    - the efficiency consequences of increasing or decreasing the number of different types of products produced, promoted, and distributed
- Optimum factor allocation
    - output elasticity of factor costs
    - marginal revenue product
    - marginal resource cost
- Pricing
    - various aspects of the pricing decision
- Transfer pricing
    - selling within a multi-divisional company
- Joint product pricing
    - price setting when two products are linked
- Price discrimination

- - different prices to different buyers
  - types of price discrimination
  - yield management
- Price skimming
  - price discrimination over time
- Two part tariffs
  - charging a price composed of two parts, usually an initial fee and an ongoing fee
- Price points
  - the effects of a non-linear demand curve on pricing
- Cost-plus pricing
  - a markup is applied to a cost term in order to calculate price
  - cost-plus pricing with elasticity considerations
  - cost plus pricing is often used along with break even analysis
- Rate of return pricing
  - calculate price based on the required rate of return on investment, or rate of return on sales
- Profit maximization
  - determining the optimum price and quantity
  - the totals approach
  - marginal approach of production

Chapter 1. The Foundations of Entrepreneurship

a. Pricing
b. Markup
c. Price floor
d. Topics

29.   A _____ is a business that is privately owned and operated, with a small number of employees and relatively low volume of sales. The legal definition of 'small' often varies by country and industry, but is generally under 100 employees in the United States and under 50 employees in the European Union. In comparison, the definition of mid-sized business by the number of employees is generally under 500 in the U.S. and 250 for the European Union.

a. Pre-determined overhead rate
b. Golden Boot Compensation
c. Critical Success Factor
d. Small business

30.   _____ generally refers to a list of all planned expenses and revenues. It is a plan for saving and spending. A _____ is an important concept in microeconomics, which uses a _____ line to illustrate the trade-offs between two or more goods.

a. 33 Strategies of War
b. 1990 Clean Air Act
c. Budget
d. 28-hour day

31.   A _____ is a set of exclusive rights granted by a state to an inventor or his assignee for a limited period of time in exchange for a disclosure of an invention.

The procedure for granting _____s, the requirements placed on the _____ee and the extent of the exclusive rights vary widely between countries according to national laws and international agreements. Typically, however, a _____ application must include one or more claims defining the invention which must be new, inventive, and useful or industrially applicable.

a. Food, Drug, and Cosmetic Act
b. Patent
c. Federal Trade Commission Act
d. Labor Management Reporting and Disclosure Act

32.   The _____ is a performance management tool for measuring whether the smaller-scale operational activities of a company are aligned with its larger-scale objectives in terms of vision and strategy.

By focusing not only on financial outcomes but also on the operational, marketing and developmental inputs to these, the _____ helps provide a more comprehensive view of a business, which in turn helps organizations act in their best long-term interests. This tool is also being used to address business response to climate change and greenhouse gas emissions.

a. Middle management
b. Balanced scorecard
c. Management development
d. Commercial management

33.   _____ is an organization's process of defining its strategy and making decisions on allocating its resources to pursue this strategy, including its capital and people. Various business analysis techniques can be used in _____, including SWOT analysis (Strengths, Weaknesses, Opportunities, and Threats) and PEST analysis (Political, Economic, Social, and Technological analysis) or STEER analysis involving Socio-cultural, Technological, Economic, Ecological, and Regulatory factors and EPISTEL (Environment, Political, Informatic, Social, Technological, Economic and Legal)

Chapter 1. The Foundations of Entrepreneurship

_____ is the formal consideration of an organization's future course. All _____ deals with at least one of three key questions:

1. 'What do we do?'
2. 'For whom do we do it?'
3. 'How do we excel?'

In business _____, the third question is better phrased 'How can we beat or avoid competition?'. (Bradford and Duncan, page 1.)

a. 33 Strategies of War
b. 28-hour day
c. Strategic planning
d. 1990 Clean Air Act

34. _____ is an integrated communications-based process through which individuals and communities discover that existing and newly-identified needs and wants may be satisfied by the products and services of others.

_____ is defined by the American _____ Association as the activity, set of institutions, and processes for creating, communicating, delivering, and exchanging offerings that have value for customers, clients, partners, and society at large. The term developed from the original meaning which referred literally to going to market, as in shopping, or going to a market to buy or sell goods or services.

a. Market development
b. Marketing
c. Customer relationship management
d. Disruptive technology

35. _____ is one of the four Ps of the marketing mix. The other three aspects are product, promotion, and place. It is also a key variable in microeconomic price allocation theory.

a. Price floor
b. Penetration pricing
c. Transfer pricing
d. Pricing

36. In a human resources context, _____ or labor _____ is the rate at which an employer gains and loses employees. Simple ways to describe it are 'how long employees tend to stay' or 'the rate of traffic through the revolving door.' _____ is measured for individual companies and for their industry as a whole. If an employer is said to have a high _____ relative to its competitors, it means that employees of that company have a shorter average tenure than those of other companies in the same industry.

a. Continuous
b. Turnover
c. Career portfolios
d. Ten year occupational employment projection

37. _____ are formal records of the financial activities of a business, person, or other entity. In British English, including United Kingdom company law, _____ are often referred to as accounts, although the term _____ is also used, particularly by accountants.

_____ provide an overview of a business or person's financial condition in both short and long term.

a. 28-hour day
b. 1990 Clean Air Act
c. Financial statements
d. 33 Strategies of War

38. _____ refers to a range of skills, tools, and techniques used to manage time when accomplishing specific tasks, projects and goals. This set encompass a wide scope of activities, and these include planning, allocating, setting goals, delegation, analysis of time spent, monitoring, organizing, scheduling, and prioritizing. Initially _____ referred to just business or work activities, but eventually the term broadened to include personal activities also.

a. Voice of the customer
b. Time management
c. Cash cow
d. Formula for Change

Chapter 2. Inside the Entrepreneurial Mind: From Ideas to Reality

1. _____ according to Onuoha (2007) is the practice of starting new organizations or revitalizing mature organizations, particularly new businesses generally in response to identified opportunities. _____ is often a difficult undertaking, as a vast majority of new businesses fail. Entrepreneurial activities are substantially different depending on the type of organization that is being started.
    a. A Stake in the Outcome
    b. A4e
    c. AAAI
    d. Entrepreneurship

2. The _____ is a performance management tool for measuring whether the smaller-scale operational activities of a company are aligned with its larger-scale objectives in terms of vision and strategy.

    By focusing not only on financial outcomes but also on the operational, marketing and developmental inputs to these, the _____ helps provide a more comprehensive view of a business, which in turn helps organizations act in their best long-term interests. This tool is also being used to address business response to climate change and greenhouse gas emissions.

    a. Middle management
    b. Balanced scorecard
    c. Management development
    d. Commercial management

3. In business and engineering, _____ is the term used to describe the complete process of bringing a new product or service to market. There are two parallel paths involved in the _____ process: one involves the idea generation, product design, and detail engineering; the other involves market research and marketing analysis. Companies typically see _____ as the first stage in generating and commercializing new products within the overall strategic process of product life cycle management used to maintain or grow their market share.
    a. 33 Strategies of War
    b. 28-hour day
    c. 1990 Clean Air Act
    d. New product development

4. In business and engineering, new _____ is the term used to describe the complete process of bringing a new product or service to market. There are two parallel paths involved in the NProduct development process: one involves the idea generation, product design, and detail engineering; the other involves market research and marketing analysis. Companies typically see new _____ as the first stage in generating and commercializing new products within the overall strategic process of product life cycle management used to maintain or grow their market share.
    a. 1990 Clean Air Act
    b. 33 Strategies of War
    c. 28-hour day
    d. Product development

5. A _____ is a professional who provides advice in a particular area of expertise such as management, accountancy, the environment, entertainment, technology, law , human resources, marketing, medicine, finance, economics, public affairs, communication, engineering, sound system design, graphic design, or waste management.

    A _____ is usually an expert or a professional in a specific field and has a wide knowledge of the subject matter. A _____ usually works for a consultancy firm or is self-employed, and engages with multiple and changing clients.

    a. 1990 Clean Air Act
    b. 28-hour day
    c. Consultant
    d. 33 Strategies of War

6. _____ is the state or fact of exclusive rights and control over property, which may be an object, land/real estate or intellectual property. An _____ right is also referred to as title. The concept of _____ has existed for thousands of years and in all cultures.
   a. Emanation of the state
   b. A Stake in the Outcome
   c. A4e
   d. Ownership

7. The 'business case for _____', theorizes that in a global marketplace, a company that employs a diverse workforce (both men and women, people of many generations, people from ethnically and racially diverse backgrounds etc.) is better able to understand the demographics of the marketplace it serves and is thus better equipped to thrive in that marketplace than a company that has a more limited range of employee demographics.

An additional corollary suggests that a company that supports the _____ of its workforce can also improve employee satisfaction, productivity and retention.

   a. Trademark
   b. Virtual team
   c. Kanban
   d. Diversity

8. _____ is a term used for a number of concepts involving either the performance of an investigation of a business or person, or the performance of an act with a certain standard of care. It can be a legal obligation, but the term will more commonly apply to voluntary investigations. A common example of _____ in various industries is the process through which a potential acquirer evaluates a target company or its assets for acquisition.
   a. Technology transfer
   b. Due diligence
   c. Flextime
   d. Negligence in employment

9. _____ refers to the methods of practicing and using another person's business philosophy. The franchisor grants the independent operator the right to distribute its products, techniques, and trademarks for a percentage of gross monthly sales and a royalty fee. Various tangibles and intangibles such as national or international advertising, training, and other support services are commonly made available by the franchisor.
   a. Franchising
   b. 1990 Clean Air Act
   c. 28-hour day
   d. ServiceMaster

10. The phrase mergers and _____s refers to the aspect of corporate strategy, corporate finance and management dealing with the buying, selling and combining of different companies that can aid, finance, or help a growing company in a given industry grow rapidly without having to create another business entity.

An _____, also known as a takeover or a buyout, is the buying of one company (the 'target') by another. An _____ may be friendly or hostile.

   a. A Stake in the Outcome
   b. A4e
   c. Acquisition
   d. AAAI

Chapter 2. Inside the Entrepreneurial Mind: From Ideas to Reality

11. _____ is a process and a set of procedures used to estimate the economic value of an owner's interest in a business. Valuation is used by financial market participants to determine the price they are willing to pay or receive to consummate a sale of a business. In addition to estimating the selling price of a business, the same valuation tools are often used by business appraisers to resolve disputes related to estate and gift taxation, divorce litigation, allocate business purchase price among business assets, establish a formula for estimating the value of partners' ownership interest for buy-sell agreements, and many other business and legal purposes.
   a. No-FEAR Act
   b. Munn v. Illinois
   c. Robinson-Patman Act
   d. Business valuation

12. _____, commonly known as e-commerce, consists of the buying and selling of products or services over electronic systems such as the Internet and other computer networks. The amount of trade conducted electronically has grown extraordinarily with widespread Internet usage. The use of commerce is conducted in this way, spurring and drawing on innovations in electronic funds transfer, supply chain management, Internet marketing, online transaction processing, electronic data interchange (EDI), inventory management systems, and automated data collection systems.
   a. Electronic Commerce
   b. A Stake in the Outcome
   c. Online shopping
   d. A4e

13. _____ has been described as the 'process of social influence in which one person can enlist the aid and support of others in the accomplishment of a common task' . A definition more inclusive of followers comes from Alan Keith of Genentech who said '_____ is ultimately about creating a way for people to contribute to making something extraordinary happen.'

   _____ is one of the most salient aspects of the organizational context. However, defining _____ has been challenging.

   a. Leadership
   b. 1990 Clean Air Act
   c. 28-hour day
   d. Situational leadership

14. An _____ is a person who has possession of an enterprise and assumes significant accountability for the inherent risks and the outcome. It is an ambitious leader who combines land, labor, and capital to create and market new goods or services. The term is a loanword from French and was first defined by the Irish economist Richard Cantillon.
   a. A4e
   b. A Stake in the Outcome
   c. AAAI
   d. Entrepreneur

15. _____ is a group creativity technique designed to generate a large number of ideas for the solution of a problem. The method was first popularized in the late 1930s by Alex Faickney Osborn in a book called Applied Imagination. Osborn proposed that groups could double their creative output with _____.
   a. Affiliation
   b. Adam Smith
   c. Abraham Harold Maslow
   d. Brainstorming

16. _____ is the automatic construction of physical objects using solid freeform fabrication. The first techniques for _____ became available in the late 1980s and were used to produce models and prototype parts. Today, they are used for a much wider range of applications and are even used to manufacture production quality parts in relatively small numbers.

a. 1990 Clean Air Act
b. 28-hour day
c. Rapid prototyping
d. 33 Strategies of War

17. In the United States, a _____ is a patent granted on the ornamental design of a functional item. _____s are a type of industrial design right. Ornamental designs of jewelry, furniture, beverage containers (see Fig.
   a. Reverification
   b. Robinson-Patman Act
   c. Smith Report
   d. Design patent

18. _____ , also referred to simply as a 'public offering' or 'flotation,' is when a company issues common stock or shares to the public for the first time. They are often issued by smaller, younger companies seeking capital to expand, but can also be done by large privately-owned companies looking to become publicly traded.

In an _____ the issuer may obtain the assistance of an underwriting firm, which helps it determine what type of security to issue (common or preferred), best offering price and time to bring it to market.

   a. Occupational Safety and Health Administration
   b. Outsourcing
   c. Initial public offering
   d. Unemployment insurance

19. _____ are legal property rights over creations of the mind, both artistic and commercial, and the corresponding fields of law. Under _____ law, owners are granted certain exclusive rights to a variety of intangible assets, such as musical, literary, and artistic works; ideas, discoveries and inventions; and words, phrases, symbols, and designs. Common types of _____ include copyrights, trademarks, patents, industrial design rights and trade secrets.
   a. Intent
   b. Intellectual property
   c. Unemployment Action Center
   d. Equal Pay Act

20. A _____ is a set of exclusive rights granted by a state to an inventor or his assignee for a limited period of time in exchange for a disclosure of an invention.

The procedure for granting _____s, the requirements placed on the _____ee and the extent of the exclusive rights vary widely between countries according to national laws and international agreements. Typically, however, a _____ application must include one or more claims defining the invention which must be new, inventive, and useful or industrially applicable.

   a. Labor Management Reporting and Disclosure Act
   b. Food, Drug, and Cosmetic Act
   c. Federal Trade Commission Act
   d. Patent

21. In economics, _____ is a measure of the relative satisfaction from consumption of various goods and services. Given this measure, one may speak meaningfully of increasing or decreasing _____, and thereby explain economic behavior in terms of attempts to increase one's _____. For illustrative purposes, changes in _____ are sometimes expressed in units called utils.
   a. Indirect utility function
   b. Ordinal utility
   c. A Stake in the Outcome
   d. Utility

22. _____ plant, and equipment, is a term used in accountancy for assets and property which cannot easily be converted into cash. This can be compared with current assets such as cash or bank accounts, which are described as liquid assets. In most cases, only tangible assets are referred to as fixed.

a. 33 Strategies of War
c. 28-hour day
b. 1990 Clean Air Act
d. Fixed asset

23. _____ is an advertisement in which a particular product specifically mentions a competitor by name for the express purpose of showing why the competitor is inferior to the product naming it.

This should not be confused with parody advertisements, where a fictional product is being advertised for the purpose of poking fun at the particular advertisement, nor should it be confused with the use of a coined brand name for the purpose of comparing the product without actually naming an actual competitor. ('Wikipedia tastes better and is less filling than the Encyclopedia Galactica.')

In the 1980s, during what has been referred to as the cola wars, soft-drink manufacturer Pepsi ran a series of advertisements where people, caught on hidden camera, in a blind taste test, chose Pepsi over rival Coca-Cola.

a. Comparative advertising
c. 33 Strategies of War
b. 1990 Clean Air Act
d. 28-hour day

24. A _____ is a distinctive sign or indicator used by an individual, business organization, or other legal entity to identify that the products and/or services to consumers with which the _____ appears originate from a unique source and to distinguish its products or services from those of other entities.
a. Succession planning
c. Trademark
b. Kanban
d. Virtual team

Chapter 3. Designing a Competitive Business Model and Building a Solid Strategic Plan

1. _____ is an organization's process of defining its strategy and making decisions on allocating its resources to pursue this strategy, including its capital and people. Various business analysis techniques can be used in _____, including SWOT analysis (Strengths, Weaknesses, Opportunities, and Threats) and PEST analysis (Political, Economic, Social, and Technological analysis) or STEER analysis involving Socio-cultural, Technological, Economic, Ecological, and Regulatory factors and EPISTEL (Environment, Political, Informatic, Social, Technological, Economic and Legal)

_____ is the formal consideration of an organization's future course. All _____ deals with at least one of three key questions:

   1. 'What do we do?'
   2. 'For whom do we do it?'
   3. 'How do we excel?'

In business _____, the third question is better phrased 'How can we beat or avoid competition?'. (Bradford and Duncan, page 1.)

   a. 1990 Clean Air Act
   b. Strategic planning
   c. 33 Strategies of War
   d. 28-hour day

2. A _____ is a formal statement of a set of business goals, the reasons why they are believed attainable, and the plan for reaching those goals. It may also contain background information about the organization or team attempting to reach those goals.

The business goals may be defined for for-profit or for non-profit organizations.

   a. Business plan
   b. Distributed management
   c. Time management
   d. Crisis management

3. _____ refers to the stock of skills and knowledge embodied in the ability to perform labor so as to produce economic value. It is the skills and knowledge gained by a worker through education and experience. Many early economic theories refer to it simply as labor, one of three factors of production, and consider it to be a fungible resource -- homogeneous and easily interchangeable.
   a. Productivity management
   b. Market structure
   c. Deflation
   d. Human capital

4. _____ , also referred to simply as a 'public offering' or 'flotation,' is when a company issues common stock or shares to the public for the first time. They are often issued by smaller, younger companies seeking capital to expand, but can also be done by large privately-owned companies looking to become publicly traded.

In an _____ the issuer may obtain the assistance of an underwriting firm, which helps it determine what type of security to issue (common or preferred), best offering price and time to bring it to market.

   a. Unemployment insurance
   b. Outsourcing
   c. Occupational Safety and Health Administration
   d. Initial public offering

Chapter 3. Designing a Competitive Business Model and Building a Solid Strategic Plan

5. The term _____ collectively refers to all resources that determine the value and the competitiveness of an enterprise. As such, it includes as subsets the attributes that concur to building all financial statements as well as the balance sheet.

    a. AAAI
    b. A4e
    c. A Stake in the Outcome
    d. Intellectual capital

6. _____ is, in very basic words, a position a firm occupies against its competitors.

According to Michael Porter, the three methods for creating a sustainable _____ are through:

1. Cost leadership

2. Differentiation

3. Focus (economics)

    a. 28-hour day
    b. 1990 Clean Air Act
    c. Theory Z
    d. Competitive advantage

7. _____ is something that a firm can do well and that meets the following three conditions:

Competencies are things that companys execute well across several business units or product sectors.

Firms usually have few competencies, but these are usually less liable to change rapidly.

   1. It provides consumer benefits
   2. It is not easy for competitors to imitate
   3. It can be leveraged widely to many products and markets.

A _____ can take various forms, including technical/subject matter know-how, a reliable process and/or close relationships with customers and suppliers (Mascarenhas et al. 1998.)

   a. Dominant Design
   b. NAIRU
   c. Core competency
   d. Learning-by-doing

8. Competitive advantage is, in very basic words, a position a firm occupies against its competitors.

According to Michael Porter, the three methods for creating a _____ are through:

1. Cost leadership - Cost advantage occurs when a firm delivers the same services as its competitors but at a lower cost;

2.

Chapter 3. Designing a Competitive Business Model and Building a Solid Strategic Plan

a. Theory Z
b. Sustainable competitive advantage
c. 28-hour day
d. 1990 Clean Air Act

9. A _____ is a professional who provides advice in a particular area of expertise such as management, accountancy, the environment, entertainment, technology, law, human resources, marketing, medicine, finance, economics, public affairs, communication, engineering, sound system design, graphic design, or waste management.

A _____ is usually an expert or a professional in a specific field and has a wide knowledge of the subject matter. A _____ usually works for a consultancy firm or is self-employed, and engages with multiple and changing clients.

a. 1990 Clean Air Act
b. 28-hour day
c. 33 Strategies of War
d. Consultant

10. _____ is the state or fact of exclusive rights and control over property, which may be an object, land/real estate or intellectual property. An _____ right is also referred to as title. The concept of _____ has existed for thousands of years and in all cultures.

a. A Stake in the Outcome
b. Ownership
c. A4e
d. Emanation of the state

11. The phrase mergers and _____s refers to the aspect of corporate strategy, corporate finance and management dealing with the buying, selling and combining of different companies that can aid, finance, or help a growing company in a given industry grow rapidly without having to create another business entity.

An _____, also known as a takeover or a buyout, is the buying of one company (the 'target') by another. An _____ may be friendly or hostile.

a. AAAI
b. A Stake in the Outcome
c. A4e
d. Acquisition

12. A _____ is a brief written statement of the purpose of a company or organization. Ideally, a _____ guides the actions of the organization, spells out its overall goal, provides a sense of direction, and guides decision making for all levels of management.

_____s often contain the following:

- Purpose and aim of the organization
- The organization's primary stakeholders: clients, stockholders, etc.
- Responsibilities of the organization toward these stakeholders
- Products and services offered

20   Chapter 3. Designing a Competitive Business Model and Building a Solid Strategic Plan

In developing a _____:

- Encourage as much input as feasible from employees, volunteers, and other stakeholders
- Publicize it broadly

The _____ can be used to resolve differences between business stakeholders. Stakeholders include: employees including managers and executives, stockholders, board of directors, customers, suppliers, distributors, creditors, governments (local, state, federal, etc.), unions, competitors, NGO's, and the general public.

a. 33 Strategies of War
c. 28-hour day
b. Mission statement
d. 1990 Clean Air Act

13. _____ is a strategic planning method used to evaluate the Strengths, Weaknesses, Opportunities, and Threats involved in a project or in a business venture. It involves specifying the objective of the business venture or project and identifying the internal and external factors that are favorable and unfavorable to achieving that objective. The technique is credited to Albert Humphrey, who led a convention at Stanford University in the 1960s and 1970s using data from Fortune 500 companies.

a. Corporate image
c. SWOT analysis
b. Marketing
d. Market share

14. _____ is one of the managerial functions like planning, organizing, staffing and directing. It is an important function because it helps to check the errors and to take the corrective action so that deviation from standards are minimized and stated goals of the organization are achieved in desired manner. According to modern concepts, _____ is a foreseeing action whereas earlier concept of _____ was used only when errors were detected. _____ in management means setting standards, measuring actual performance and taking corrective action.

a. Turnover
c. Schedule of reinforcement
b. Decision tree pruning
d. Control

15. _____ has been described as the 'process of social influence in which one person can enlist the aid and support of others in the accomplishment of a common task' . A definition more inclusive of followers comes from Alan Keith of Genentech who said '_____ is ultimately about creating a way for people to contribute to making something extraordinary happen.'

_____ is one of the most salient aspects of the organizational context. However, defining _____ has been challenging.

a. 1990 Clean Air Act
c. Leadership
b. 28-hour day
d. Situational leadership

Chapter 3. Designing a Competitive Business Model and Building a Solid Strategic Plan   21

16. _____ is a process of planning and controlling the performance or execution of any type of activity, such as:

- a project (project _____) or
- a process (process _____, sometimes referred to as the process performance measurement and management system.)

Organization's senior management is responsible for carrying out its _____.

a. Human Relations Movement
c. Work design
b. Participatory management
d. Management process

17. In finance, an _____ is a contract between a buyer and a seller that gives the buyer the right--but not the obligation--to buy or to sell a particular asset (the underlying asset) at a later day at an agreed price. In return for granting the _____, the seller collects a payment (the premium) from the buyer. A call _____ gives the buyer the right to buy the underlying asset; a put _____ gives the buyer of the _____ the right to sell the underlying asset.

a. A Stake in the Outcome
c. A4e
b. AAAI
d. Option

18. _____ according to Onuoha (2007) is the practice of starting new organizations or revitalizing mature organizations, particularly new businesses generally in response to identified opportunities. _____ is often a difficult undertaking, as a vast majority of new businesses fail. Entrepreneurial activities are substantially different depending on the type of organization that is being started.

a. Entrepreneurship
c. A Stake in the Outcome
b. A4e
d. AAAI

19. _____, commonly known as e-commerce, consists of the buying and selling of products or services over electronic systems such as the Internet and other computer networks. The amount of trade conducted electronically has grown extraordinarily with widespread Internet usage. The use of commerce is conducted in this way, spurring and drawing on innovations in electronic funds transfer, supply chain management, Internet marketing, online transaction processing, electronic data interchange (EDI), inventory management systems, and automated data collection systems.

a. A4e
c. Online shopping
b. A Stake in the Outcome
d. Electronic Commerce

20. _____ consists of the mental process of thinking involved with the process of judging the merits of multiple options and selecting one of them for action. Some simple examples include deciding whether to get up in the morning or go back to sleep, or selecting a given route for a journey. More complex examples (often decisions that affect what a person thinks or their core beliefs) include choosing a lifestyle, religious affiliation, or political position.

a. Groups decision making
c. Trade study
b. Championship mobilization
d. Choice

21. A broad definition of _____ is the action of gathering, analyzing, and distributing information about products, customers, competitors and any aspect of the environment needed to support executives and managers in making strategic decisions for an organization.

Chapter 3. Designing a Competitive Business Model and Building a Solid Strategic Plan

Key points of this definitions:

1. _____ is an ethical and legal business practice. (This is important as _____ professionals emphasize that the discipline is not the same as industrial espionage which is both unethical and usually illegal.)
2. The focus is on the external business environment.
3. There is a process involved in gathering information, converting it into intelligence and then utilizing this in business decision making. _____ professionals emphasize that if the intelligence gathered is not usable (or actionable) then it is not intelligence.

A more focused definition of _____ regards it as the organizational function responsible for the early identification of risks and opportunities in the market before they become obvious. Experts also call this process the early signal analysis. This definition focuses attention on the difference between dissemination of widely available factual information (such as market statistics, financial reports, newspaper clippings) performed by functions such as libraries and information centers, and _____ which is a perspective on developments and events aimed at yielding a competitive edge.

a. 28-hour day
b. 1990 Clean Air Act
c. Competitive intelligence
d. Competitor or Competitive Intelligence

22. _____ comprises a range of practices used in an organisation to identify, create, represent, distribute and enable adoption of insights and experiences. Such insights and experiences comprise knowledge, either embodied in individuals or embedded in organisational processes or practice.

An established discipline since 1991, _____ includes courses taught in the fields of business administration, information systems, management, and library and information sciences.

a. 28-hour day
b. 1990 Clean Air Act
c. 33 Strategies of War
d. Knowledge management

23. The _____ is a performance management tool for measuring whether the smaller-scale operational activities of a company are aligned with its larger-scale objectives in terms of vision and strategy.

By focusing not only on financial outcomes but also on the operational, marketing and developmental inputs to these, the _____ helps provide a more comprehensive view of a business, which in turn helps organizations act in their best long-term interests. This tool is also being used to address business response to climate change and greenhouse gas emissions.

a. Management development
b. Commercial management
c. Middle management
d. Balanced scorecard

Chapter 3. Designing a Competitive Business Model and Building a Solid Strategic Plan 23

24. The 'business case for _____', theorizes that in a global marketplace, a company that employs a diverse workforce (both men and women, people of many generations, people from ethnically and racially diverse backgrounds etc.) is better able to understand the demographics of the marketplace it serves and is thus better equipped to thrive in that marketplace than a company that has a more limited range of employee demographics.

An additional corollary suggests that a company that supports the _____ of its workforce can also improve employee satisfaction, productivity and retention.

   a. Virtual team
   c. Kanban
   b. Trademark
   d. Diversity

25. In economics, business, retail, and accounting, a _____ is the value of money that has been used up to produce something, and hence is not available for use anymore. In economics, a _____ is an alternative that is given up as a result of a decision. In business, the _____ may be one of acquisition, in which case the amount of money expended to acquire it is counted as _____.
   a. Fixed costs
   c. Cost allocation
   b. Cost overrun
   d. Cost

26. _____ is a concept developed by Michael Porter, used in business strategy. It describes a way to establish the competitive advantage. _____, in basic words, means the lowest cost of operation in the industry.
   a. Switching cost
   c. Strategic business unit
   b. Strategic group
   d. Cost leadership

Chapter 4. Conducting a Feasibility Analysis and Crafting a Winning Business Plan

1. A _____ is a formal statement of a set of business goals, the reasons why they are believed attainable, and the plan for reaching those goals. It may also contain background information about the organization or team attempting to reach those goals.

The business goals may be defined for for-profit or for non-profit organizations.

- a. Crisis management
- b. Distributed management
- c. Time management
- d. Business plan

2. A _____ is a documented investigation of a Market that is used to inform a firm's planning activities particularly around decision of: inventory, purchase, work force expansion/contraction, facility expansion, purchases of capital equipment, promotional activities, and many other aspects of a company.

Not all managers are asked to conduct a _____, but all managers must make decisions using _____ data and understand how the data was derived. So all managers need a reasonable understanding of the tools most used for making sales forecasts and analyzing markets.

- a. Market analysis
- b. Marketing research process
- c. 1990 Clean Air Act
- d. Marketing research

3. _____ is a concept related to the relative abilities of parties in a situation to exert influence over each other. If both parties are on an equal footing in a debate, then they will have equal _____, such as in a perfectly competitive market, or between an evenly matched monopoly and monopsony.

There are a number of fields where the concept of _____ has proven crucial to coherent analysis: game theory, labour economics, collective bargaining arrangements, diplomatic negotiations, settlement of litigation, the price of insurance, and any negotiation in general.

- a. Trade credit
- b. 1990 Clean Air Act
- c. Buy-sell agreement
- d. Bargaining power

4. _____ is, in very basic words, a position a firm occupies against its competitors.

According to Michael Porter, the three methods for creating a sustainable _____ are through:

1. Cost leadership

2. Differentiation

3. Focus (economics)

- a. 28-hour day
- b. 1990 Clean Air Act
- c. Theory Z
- d. Competitive advantage

5. The _____ is a performance management tool for measuring whether the smaller-scale operational activities of a company are aligned with its larger-scale objectives in terms of vision and strategy.

Chapter 4. Conducting a Feasibility Analysis and Crafting a Winning Business Plan

By focusing not only on financial outcomes but also on the operational, marketing and developmental inputs to these, the _____ helps provide a more comprehensive view of a business, which in turn helps organizations act in their best long-term interests. This tool is also being used to address business response to climate change and greenhouse gas emissions.

  a. Management development
  c. Commercial management
  b. Middle management
  d. Balanced scorecard

6. A _____ is a professional who provides advice in a particular area of expertise such as management, accountancy, the environment, entertainment, technology, law , human resources, marketing, medicine, finance, economics, public affairs, communication, engineering, sound system design, graphic design, or waste management.

A _____ is usually an expert or a professional in a specific field and has a wide knowledge of the subject matter. A _____ usually works for a consultancy firm or is self-employed, and engages with multiple and changing clients.

  a. 33 Strategies of War
  c. 1990 Clean Air Act
  b. 28-hour day
  d. Consultant

7. _____ consists of the mental process of thinking involved with the process of judging the merits of multiple options and selecting one of them for action. Some simple examples include deciding whether to get up in the morning or go back to sleep, or selecting a given route for a journey. More complex examples (often decisions that affect what a person thinks or their core beliefs) include choosing a lifestyle, religious affiliation, or political position.

  a. Groups decision making
  c. Championship mobilization
  b. Trade study
  d. Choice

8. _____ is the state or fact of exclusive rights and control over property, which may be an object, land/real estate or intellectual property. An _____ right is also referred to as title. The concept of _____ has existed for thousands of years and in all cultures.

  a. A4e
  c. Ownership
  b. Emanation of the state
  d. A Stake in the Outcome

9. _____ or _____ data refers to selected population characteristics as used in government, marketing or opinion research, or the _____ profiles used in such research. Note the distinction from the term 'demography' Commonly-used _____s include race, age, income, disabilities, mobility (in terms of travel time to work or number of vehicles available), educational attainment, home ownership, employment status, and even location.

  a. Adam Smith
  c. Abraham Harold Maslow
  b. Affiliation
  d. Demographic

10. A _____ is a form of qualitative research in which a group of people are asked about their attitude towards a product, service, concept, advertisement, idea, or packaging. Questions are asked in an interactive group setting where participants are free to talk with other group members.

The first _____s were created at the Bureau of Applied Social Research by associate director, sociologist Robert K. Merton.

Chapter 4. Conducting a Feasibility Analysis and Crafting a Winning Business Plan

a. Marketing research
b. 1990 Clean Air Act
c. Market analysis
d. Focus group

11. Marketing research is a form of business research and is generally divided into two categories: consumer _____ and business-to-business (B2B) _____, which was previously known as industrial marketing research. Consumer marketing research studies the buying habits of individual people while business-to-business marketing research investigates the markets for products sold by one business to another.

Consumer _____ is a form of applied sociology that concentrates on understanding the behaviours, whims and preferences, of consumers in a market-based economy, and aims to understand the effects and comparative success of marketing campaigns.

a. Questionnaire construction
b. Market research
c. Questionnaire
d. Mystery shoppers

12. An _____ is an organization founded and funded by businesses that operate in a specific industry. An industry trade association participates in public relations activities such as advertising, education, political donations, lobbying and publishing, but its main focus is collaboration between companies, or standardization. Associations may offer other services, such as producing conferences, networking or charitable events or offering classes or educational materials.

a. Industry trade group
b. A4e
c. A Stake in the Outcome
d. AAAI

13. The phrase mergers and _____s refers to the aspect of corporate strategy, corporate finance and management dealing with the buying, selling and combining of different companies that can aid, finance, or help a growing company in a given industry grow rapidly without having to create another business entity.

An _____, also known as a takeover or a buyout, is the buying of one company (the 'target') by another. An _____ may be friendly or hostile.

a. A Stake in the Outcome
b. A4e
c. AAAI
d. Acquisition

14. _____, commonly known as e-commerce, consists of the buying and selling of products or services over electronic systems such as the Internet and other computer networks. The amount of trade conducted electronically has grown extraordinarily with widespread Internet usage. The use of commerce is conducted in this way, spurring and drawing on innovations in electronic funds transfer, supply chain management, Internet marketing, online transaction processing, electronic data interchange (EDI), inventory management systems, and automated data collection systems.

a. A4e
b. Electronic Commerce
c. Online shopping
d. A Stake in the Outcome

15. A _____ is a research instrument consisting of a series of questions and other prompts for the purpose of gathering information from respondents. Although they are often designed for statistical analysis of the responses, this is not always the case. The _____ was invented by Sir Francis Galton.

a. Mystery shoppers
b. Structured interview
c. Questionnaire construction
d. Questionnaire

Chapter 4. Conducting a Feasibility Analysis and Crafting a Winning Business Plan

16. _____ is the process of estimation in unknown situations. Prediction is a similar, but more general term. Both can refer to estimation of time series, cross-sectional or longitudinal data.
    a. 1990 Clean Air Act
    b. 33 Strategies of War
    c. 28-hour day
    d. Forecasting

17. _____ refers to the movement of cash into or out of a business or financial product. It is usually measured during a specified, finite period of time. Measurement of _____ can be used

    - to determine a project's rate of return or value. The time of _____s into and out of projects are used as inputs in financial models such as internal rate of return, and net present value.
    - to determine problems with a business's liquidity. Being profitable does not necessarily mean being liquid. A company can fail because of a shortage of cash, even while profitable.
    - as an alternate measure of a business's profits when it is believed that accrual accounting concepts do not represent economic realities. For example, a company may be notionally profitable but generating little operational cash (as may be the case for a company that barters its products rather than selling for cash.) In such a case, the company may be deriving additional operating cash by issuing shares evaluating default risk, re-investment requirements, etc.

    _____ is a generic term used differently depending on the context. It may be defined by users for their own purposes.

    a. Gross profit margin
    b. Gross profit
    c. Cash flow
    d. Sweat equity

18. _____ is a process and a set of procedures used to estimate the economic value of an owner's interest in a business. Valuation is used by financial market participants to determine the price they are willing to pay or receive to consummate a sale of a business. In addition to estimating the selling price of a business, the same valuation tools are often used by business appraisers to resolve disputes related to estate and gift taxation, divorce litigation, allocate business purchase price among business assets, establish a formula for estimating the value of partners' ownership interest for buy-sell agreements, and many other business and legal purposes.
    a. No-FEAR Act
    b. Munn v. Illinois
    c. Robinson-Patman Act
    d. Business valuation

19. A _____ is a brief written statement of the purpose of a company or organization. Ideally, a _____ guides the actions of the organization, spells out its overall goal, provides a sense of direction, and guides decision making for all levels of management.

    _____s often contain the following:

    - Purpose and aim of the organization
    - The organization's primary stakeholders: clients, stockholders, etc.
    - Responsibilities of the organization toward these stakeholders
    - Products and services offered

Chapter 4. Conducting a Feasibility Analysis and Crafting a Winning Business Plan

In developing a _____:

- Encourage as much input as feasible from employees, volunteers, and other stakeholders
- Publicize it broadly

The _____ can be used to resolve differences between business stakeholders. Stakeholders include: employees including managers and executives, stockholders, board of directors, customers, suppliers, distributors, creditors, governments (local, state, federal, etc.), unions, competitors, NGO's, and the general public.

a. 33 Strategies of War
b. 28-hour day
c. 1990 Clean Air Act
d. Mission statement

20. _____ refers to the aggregated strategies of single business firm or a strategic business unit (SBU) in a diversified corporation. According to Michael Porter, a firm must formulate a _____ that incorporates either cost leadership, differentiation or focus in order to achieve a sustainable competitive advantage and long-term success in its chosen arenas or industries.

Functional strategies include marketing strategies, new product development strategies, human resource strategies, financial strategies, legal strategies, supply-chain strategies, and information technology management strategies.

a. Strategic thinking
b. Competitive heterogeneity
c. Switching cost
d. Business strategy

21. _____ is an advertisement in which a particular product specifically mentions a competitor by name for the express purpose of showing why the competitor is inferior to the product naming it.

This should not be confused with parody advertisements, where a fictional product is being advertised for the purpose of poking fun at the particular advertisement, nor should it be confused with the use of a coined brand name for the purpose of comparing the product without actually naming an actual competitor. ('Wikipedia tastes better and is less filling than the Encyclopedia Galactica.')

In the 1980s, during what has been referred to as the cola wars, soft-drink manufacturer Pepsi ran a series of advertisements where people, caught on hidden camera, in a blind taste test, chose Pepsi over rival Coca-Cola.

a. 28-hour day
b. 33 Strategies of War
c. 1990 Clean Air Act
d. Comparative advertising

22. _____ is an integrated communications-based process through which individuals and communities discover that existing and newly-identified needs and wants may be satisfied by the products and services of others.

Chapter 4. Conducting a Feasibility Analysis and Crafting a Winning Business Plan

_____ is defined by the American _____ Association as the activity, set of institutions, and processes for creating, communicating, delivering, and exchanging offerings that have value for customers, clients, partners, and society at large. The term developed from the original meaning which referred literally to going to market, as in shopping, or going to a market to buy or sell goods or services.

a. Marketing
b. Market development
c. Customer relationship management
d. Disruptive technology

23. A _____ is a written document that details the necessary actions to achieve one or more marketing objectives. It can be for a product or service, a brand, or a product line. _____s cover between one and five years.
a. Market development
b. Disruptive technology
c. Marketing plan
d. Marketing strategy

24. A _____ is a process that can allow an organization to concentrate its limited resources on the greatest opportunities to increase sales and achieve a sustainable competitive advantage. A _____ should be centered around the key concept that customer satisfaction is the main goal.

A _____ is a written plan which combines product development, promotion, distribution, and pricing approach, identifies the firm's marketing goals, and explains how they will be achieved within a stated timeframe.

a. Category management
b. Disruptive technology
c. Marketing strategy
d. Product bundling

25. _____ is a form of communication that typically attempts to persuade potential customers to purchase or to consume more of a particular brand of product or service. 'While now central to the contemporary global economy and the reproduction of global production networks, it is only quite recently that _____ has been more than a marginal influence on patterns of sales and production. The formation of modern _____ was intimately bound up with the emergence of new forms of monopoly capitalism around the end of the 19th and beginning of the 20th century as one element in corporate strategies to create, organize and where possible control markets, especially for mass produced consumer goods.
a. A Stake in the Outcome
b. A4e
c. AAAI
d. Advertising

26. _____ is one of the four elements of marketing mix. An organization or set of organizations (go-betweens) involved in the process of making a product or service available for use or consumption by a consumer or business user.

The other three parts of the marketing mix are product, pricing, and promotion.

a. Distribution
b. Job creation programs
c. Missing completely at random
d. Matching theory

27. _____ is one of the four Ps of the marketing mix. The other three aspects are product, promotion, and place. It is also a key variable in microeconomic price allocation theory.
a. Pricing
b. Price floor
c. Transfer pricing
d. Penetration pricing

Chapter 4. Conducting a Feasibility Analysis and Crafting a Winning Business Plan

28. _____ in marketing and strategic management is an assessment of the strengths and weaknesses of current and potential competitors. This analysis provides both an offensive and defensive strategic context through which to identify opportunities and threats. Competitor profiling coalesces all of the relevant sources of _____ into one framework in the support of efficient and effective strategy formulation, implementation, monitoring and adjustment.
   a. Competitor or Competitive Intelligence
   b. 1990 Clean Air Act
   c. 28-hour day
   d. Competitor analysis

29. A _____ is directly responsible for managing the day-to-day operations (and profitability) of a company.

Chief Executive Officer (CEO)
   - As the top manager, the CEO is typically responsible for the entire operations of the corporation and reports directly to the chairman and board of directors. It is the CEO's responsibility to implement board decisions and initiatives and to maintain the smooth operation of the firm, with the assistance of senior management.

   a. Getting Things Done
   b. Field service management
   c. Vorstand
   d. Management team

30. _____ are formal records of the financial activities of a business, person, or other entity. In British English, including United Kingdom company law, _____ are often referred to as accounts, although the term _____ is also used, particularly by accountants.

_____ provide an overview of a business or person's financial condition in both short and long term.

   a. 1990 Clean Air Act
   b. Financial statements
   c. 33 Strategies of War
   d. 28-hour day

31. _____ is a strategic planning method used to evaluate the Strengths, Weaknesses, Opportunities, and Threats involved in a project or in a business venture. It involves specifying the objective of the business venture or project and identifying the internal and external factors that are favorable and unfavorable to achieving that objective. The technique is credited to Albert Humphrey, who led a convention at Stanford University in the 1960s and 1970s using data from Fortune 500 companies.
   a. Corporate image
   b. Market share
   c. Marketing
   d. SWOT analysis

Chapter 5. Forms of Business Ownership

1. _____ is the state or fact of exclusive rights and control over property, which may be an object, land/real estate or intellectual property. An _____ right is also referred to as title. The concept of _____ has existed for thousands of years and in all cultures.
   a. Emanation of the state
   b. A Stake in the Outcome
   c. Ownership
   d. A4e

2. A _____ is a corporation in the United States that, for Federal income tax purposes, is taxed under 26 U.S.C. § 11 and Subchapter C (26 U.S.C.
   a. C corporation
   b. 1990 Clean Air Act
   c. 33 Strategies of War
   d. 28-hour day

3. _____ is one of the managerial functions like planning, organizing, staffing and directing. It is an important function because it helps to check the errors and to take the corrective action so that deviation from standards are minimized and stated goals of the organization are achieved in desired manner.According to modern concepts, _____ is a foreseeing action whereas earlier concept of _____ was used only when errors were detected. _____ in management means setting standards, measuring actual performance and taking corrective action.
   a. Control
   b. Decision tree pruning
   c. Turnover
   d. Schedule of reinforcement

4. In economics, business, retail, and accounting, a _____ is the value of money that has been used up to produce something, and hence is not available for use anymore. In economics, a _____ is an alternative that is given up as a result of a decision. In business, the _____ may be one of acquisition, in which case the amount of money expended to acquire it is counted as _____.
   a. Cost
   b. Fixed costs
   c. Cost overrun
   d. Cost allocation

5. _____ , also referred to simply as a 'public offering' or 'flotation,' is when a company issues common stock or shares to the public for the first time. They are often issued by smaller, younger companies seeking capital to expand, but can also be done by large privately-owned companies looking to become publicly traded.

   In an _____ the issuer may obtain the assistance of an underwriting firm, which helps it determine what type of security to issue (common or preferred), best offering price and time to bring it to market.

   a. Outsourcing
   b. Initial public offering
   c. Occupational Safety and Health Administration
   d. Unemployment insurance

6. An _____, for United States federal income tax purposes, is a corporation that makes a valid election to be taxed under Subchapter S of Chapter 1 of the Internal Revenue Code.

   In general, _____s do not pay any income taxes. Instead, the corporation's income or losses are divided among and passed through to its shareholders.

   a. S corporation
   b. 1990 Clean Air Act
   c. 33 Strategies of War
   d. 28-hour day

7. _____ involves having senior executives periodically review their top executives and those in the next lower level to determine several backups for each senior position. This is important because it often takes years of grooming to develop effective senior managers. There is a critical shortage in companies of middle and top leaders for the next five years.

a. Risk management
b. Succession planning
c. Trademark
d. Kanban

8. The _____ is a performance management tool for measuring whether the smaller-scale operational activities of a company are aligned with its larger-scale objectives in terms of vision and strategy.

By focusing not only on financial outcomes but also on the operational, marketing and developmental inputs to these, the _____ helps provide a more comprehensive view of a business, which in turn helps organizations act in their best long-term interests. This tool is also being used to address business response to climate change and greenhouse gas emissions.

a. Balanced scorecard
b. Management development
c. Middle management
d. Commercial management

9. A _____ is a formal statement of a set of business goals, the reasons why they are believed attainable, and the plan for reaching those goals. It may also contain background information about the organization or team attempting to reach those goals.

The business goals may be defined for for-profit or for non-profit organizations.

a. Distributed management
b. Time management
c. Business plan
d. Crisis management

10. The _____ is a bank regulation, which sets a framework on how banks and depository institutions must handle their capital. The categorization of assets and capital is highly standardized so that it can be risk weighted. Internationally, the Basel Committee on Banking Supervision housed at the Bank for International Settlements influence each country's banking _____s.

a. 1990 Clean Air Act
b. Reserve requirement
c. Lock box
d. Capital requirement

11. A _____ is a legal document relating to the formation of a company or corporation. It is a license to form a corporation issued by state government. Its precise meaning depends upon the legal system in which it is used, but the two primary meanings are:

- In the U.S.A. a _____ is usually used as an alternative description of a corporation's articles of incorporation.
- In English and Commonwealth legal systems, a _____ is usually a simple certificate issued by the relevant government registry as confirmation of the due incorporation and valid existence of the company.

In the U.S.A. the _____ or articles of incorporation form a major constituent part of the constitutional documents of the corporation.

Chapter 5. Forms of Business Ownership

a. Toxic Substances Control Act
b. Blue sky law
c. Civil Rights Act of 1875
d. Certificate of Incorporation

12. _____ is a concept whereby a person's financial liability is limited to a fixed sum, most commonly the value of a person's investment in a company or partnership with _____. In other words, if a company with _____ is sued, then the plaintiffs are suing the company, not its owners or investors. A shareholder in a limited company is not personally liable for any of the debts of the company, other than for the value of his investment in that company.
    a. Privity
    b. Limited liability
    c. Toxic Substances Control Act
    d. Partnership

13. A _____ is a type of business entity in which partners (owners) share with each other the profits or losses of the business. _____s are often favored over corporations for taxation purposes, as the _____ structure does not generally incur a tax on profits before it is distributed to the partners (i.e. there is no dividend tax levied.) However, depending on the _____ structure and the jurisdiction in which it operates, owners of a _____ may be exposed to greater personal liability than they would as shareholders of a corporation.
    a. Due process
    b. Federal Employers Liability Act
    c. Mediation
    d. Partnership

14. A _____ also known as a sole trader, or simply proprietorship is a type of business entity which there is only one owner and he has the final word taking all desicions by himself. All debts of the business are debts of the owner and must pay from his personal possessions. This means that the owner has unlimited liabilty.
    a. Golden hello
    b. Sole proprietorship
    c. Foreign ownership
    d. Business rule

15. An _____ is a person who has possession of an enterprise and assumes significant accountability for the inherent risks and the outcome. It is an ambitious leader who combines land, labor, and capital to create and market new goods or services. The term is a loanword from French and was first defined by the Irish economist Richard Cantillon.
    a. Entrepreneur
    b. A Stake in the Outcome
    c. A4e
    d. AAAI

16. In economics and sociology, an _____ is any factor (financial or non-financial) that enables or motivates a particular course of action, or counts as a reason for preferring one choice to the alternatives. It is an expectation that encourages people to behave in a certain way. Since human beings are purposeful creatures, the study of _____ structures is central to the study of all economic activity (both in terms of individual decision-making and in terms of co-operation and competition within a larger institutional structure.)
    a. A Stake in the Outcome
    b. AAAI
    c. A4e
    d. Incentive

17. In the commercial and legal parlance of most countries, a _____ or simply a partnership, refers to an association of persons or an unincorporated company with the following major features:

- Created by agreement, proof of existence and estoppel.
- Formed by two or more persons
- The owners are all personally liable for any legal actions and debts the company may face

It is a partnership in which partners share equally in both responsibility and liability.

Chapter 5. Forms of Business Ownership

Partnerships have certain default characteristics relating to both the relationship between the individual partners and (b) the relationship between the partnership and the outside world. The former can generally be overridden by agreement between the partners, whereas the latter generally cannot be.

The assets of the business are owned on behalf of the other partners, and they are each personally liable, jointly and severally, for business debts, taxes or tortious liability.

a. National Center for Trauma-Informed Care
b. Prospero Business Suite
c. Business Roundtable
d. General partnership

18. A _____ is a form of partnership similar to a general partnership, except that in addition to one or more general partners (GPs), there are one or more limited partners (_____s.) It is a partnership in which only one partner is required to be a general partner.

The GPs are, in all major respects, in the same legal position as partners in a conventional firm, i.e. they have management control, share the right to use partnership property, share the profits of the firm in predefined proportions, and have joint and several liability for the debts of the partnership.

a. Growth capital
b. Private equity
c. Pension fund
d. Limited partnership

19. Under _____, a claimant may pursue an obligation against any one party as if they were jointly liable and it becomes the responsibility of the defendants to sort out their respective proportions of liability and payment. This means that if the claimant pursues one defendant and receives payment, that defendant must then pursue the other obligors for a contribution to their share of the liability.

_____ is most relevant in tort claims, whereby a plaintiff may recover all the damages from any of the defendants regardless of their individual share of the liability.

a. 28-hour day
b. 1990 Clean Air Act
c. Due-on-sale clause
d. Joint and several liability

20. A _____ is a relatively new executive level position at a corporation, company, organization typically reporting directly to the CEO or board of directors. The _____ is responsible for a brand's image, experience, and promise, and propagating it throughout all aspects of the company. The brand officer oversees marketing, advertising, design, public relations and customer service departments.

a. Purchasing manager
b. Director of communications
c. Chief executive officer
d. Chief brand officer

21. A _____ is a professional who provides advice in a particular area of expertise such as management, accountancy, the environment, entertainment, technology, law , human resources, marketing, medicine, finance, economics, public affairs, communication, engineering, sound system design, graphic design, or waste management.

Chapter 5. Forms of Business Ownership 35

A _____ is usually an expert or a professional in a specific field and has a wide knowledge of the subject matter. A _____ usually works for a consultancy firm or is self-employed, and engages with multiple and changing clients.

a. Consultant
c. 1990 Clean Air Act
b. 33 Strategies of War
d. 28-hour day

22. The _____ , which includes its 1976 revision called the Revised _____, is a uniform act (similar to a model statute), proposed by the National Conference of Commissioners on Uniform State Laws ('NCCUSL') for the governance of business partnerships by U.S. States. The NCCUSL promulgated the original _____ in 1916 and the most recent revision in 2001.

The NCCUSL promulgated the original _____ in 1916, which is now called the _____ (1916) or _____ (1916); a 1976 revision named the Revised _____ which is also now called the _____ (1976), _____ (1976) or RUniform Limited Partnership Act (1976); a 1985 revision named _____ (1976) with 1985 Amendments, which is also now called _____ (1985) or RUniform Limited Partnership Act (1985); and a 2001 revision that was colloquially called Re-RUniform Limited Partnership Act during the drafting process but then was officially named the _____ (2001) or _____ (2001.)

a. A Stake in the Outcome
c. Uniform Limited Partnership Act
b. A4e
d. AAAI

23. In the United Kingdom _____s are governed by the _____s Act 2000 (in England and Wales and Scotland) and the _____s Act (Northern Ireland) 2002 in Northern Ireland. A UK _____ is a Corporate body - that is to say, it has a continuing legal existence independent of its Members, as compared to a Partnership which may (in England and Wales they do not) have a legal existence dependent upon its Membership.

A UK _____'s members have a collective ('Joint') responsibility, to the extent that they may agree in an '_____ agreement', but no individual ('several') responsibility for each other's actions.

a. Compensation methods
c. Limited liability partnership
b. Small and medium enterprises
d. Chief risk officer

24. _____ is a contractual right that gives its holder the option to enter a business transaction with the owner of something, according to specified terms, before the owner is entitled to enter into that transaction with a third party. In brief, the _____ is similar in concept to a call option.

An _____ can cover almost any sort of asset, including real estate, personal property, a patent license, a screenplay, or an interest in a business.

a. 33 Strategies of War
c. 28-hour day
b. 1990 Clean Air Act
d. Right of first refusal

Chapter 5. Forms of Business Ownership

25. A _____ or reacquired stock is stock which is bought back by the issuing company, reducing the amount of outstanding stock on the open market ('open market' including insiders' holdings.)

Stock repurchases are often used as a tax-efficient method to put cash into shareholders' hands, rather than pay dividends. Sometimes, companies do this when they feel that their stock is undervalued on the open market.

- a. Generally accepted accounting principles
- b. Current liabilities
- c. Matching principle
- d. Treasury stock

26. _____ is the imposition of two or more taxes on the same income (in the case of income taxes), asset (in the case of capital taxes), or financial transaction (in the case of sales taxes.) It refers to two distinct situations:

- taxation of dividend income without relief or credit for taxes paid by the company paying the dividend on the income from which the dividend is paid. This arises in the so-called 'classical' system of corporate taxation, used in the United States.
- taxation by two or more countries of the same income, asset or transaction, for example income paid by an entity of one country to a resident of a different country. The double liability is often mitigated by tax treaties between countries.

It is not unusual for a business or individual who is resident in one country to make a taxable gain (earnings, profits) in another. This person may find that he is obliged by domestic laws to pay tax on that gain locally and pay again in the country in which the gain was made. Since this is inequitable, many nations make bilateral _____ agreements with each other.

- a. Federal Reserve Banks
- b. Federal Unemployment Tax Act
- c. Tax evasion
- d. Double taxation

27. The U.S. _____ is an independent agency of the United States government which holds primary responsibility for enforcing the federal securities laws and regulating the securities industry, the nation's stock and options exchanges, and other electronic securities markets. The SEC was created by section 4 of the Securities Exchange Act of 1934 (now codified as 15 U.S.C. Â§ 78d and commonly referred to as the 1934 Act.)

- a. 33 Strategies of War
- b. Securities and Exchange Commission
- c. 1990 Clean Air Act
- d. 28-hour day

28. The _____ is the labour pool in employment. It is generally used to describe those working for a single company or industry, but can also apply to a geographic region like a city, country, state, etc. The term generally excludes the employers or management, and implies those involved in manual labour.

- a. Pink-collar worker
- b. Work-life balance
- c. Division of labour
- d. Workforce

29. Marketing research is a form of business research and is generally divided into two categories: consumer _____ and business-to-business (B2B) _____, which was previously known as industrial marketing research. Consumer marketing research studies the buying habits of individual people while business-to-business marketing research investigates the markets for products sold by one business to another.

Chapter 5. Forms of Business Ownership

Consumer _____ is a form of applied sociology that concentrates on understanding the behaviours, whims and preferences, of consumers in a market-based economy, and aims to understand the effects and comparative success of marketing campaigns.

a. Questionnaire
b. Market research
c. Questionnaire construction
d. Mystery shoppers

30. A _____ is an entity formed between two or more parties to undertake economic activity together. The parties agree to create a new entity by both contributing equity, and they then share in the revenues, expenses, and control of the enterprise. The venture can be for one specific project only, or a continuing business relationship such as the Fuji Xerox _____.

a. Patent
b. Joint venture
c. Meritor Savings Bank v. Vinson
d. Civil Rights Act of 1991

Chapter 6. Franchising and the Entrepreneur

1. _____ refers to the methods of practicing and using another person's business philosophy. The franchisor grants the independent operator the right to distribute its products, techniques, and trademarks for a percentage of gross monthly sales and a royalty fee. Various tangibles and intangibles such as national or international advertising, training, and other support services are commonly made available by the franchisor.

   a. 28-hour day
   b. 1990 Clean Air Act
   c. Franchising
   d. ServiceMaster

2. _____ according to Onuoha (2007) is the practice of starting new organizations or revitalizing mature organizations, particularly new businesses generally in response to identified opportunities. _____ is often a difficult undertaking, as a vast majority of new businesses fail. Entrepreneurial activities are substantially different depending on the type of organization that is being started.

   a. A Stake in the Outcome
   b. A4e
   c. AAAI
   d. Entrepreneurship

3. An _____ is a person who has possession of an enterprise and assumes significant accountability for the inherent risks and the outcome. It is an ambitious leader who combines land, labor, and capital to create and market new goods or services. The term is a loanword from French and was first defined by the Irish economist Richard Cantillon.

   a. A Stake in the Outcome
   b. A4e
   c. Entrepreneur
   d. AAAI

4. _____ is a form of communication that typically attempts to persuade potential customers to purchase or to consume more of a particular brand of product or service. 'While now central to the contemporary global economy and the reproduction of global production networks, it is only quite recently that _____ has been more than a marginal influence on patterns of sales and production. The formation of modern _____ was intimately bound up with the emergence of new forms of monopoly capitalism around the end of the 19th and beginning of the 20th century as one element in corporate strategies to create, organize and where possible control markets, especially for mass produced consumer goods.

   a. A4e
   b. A Stake in the Outcome
   c. AAAI
   d. Advertising

5. A _____ is a legal document relating to the formation of a company or corporation. It is a license to form a corporation issued by state government. Its precise meaning depends upon the legal system in which it is used, but the two primary meanings are:

   - In the U.S.A. a _____ is usually used as an alternative description of a corporation's articles of incorporation.
   - In English and Commonwealth legal systems, a _____ is usually a simple certificate issued by the relevant government registry as confirmation of the due incorporation and valid existence of the company.

   In the U.S.A. the _____ or articles of incorporation form a major constituent part of the constitutional documents of the corporation.

   a. Blue sky law
   b. Civil Rights Act of 1875
   c. Certificate of Incorporation
   d. Toxic Substances Control Act

6. _____ is one of the four elements of marketing mix. An organization or set of organizations (go-betweens) involved in the process of making a product or service available for use or consumption by a consumer or business user.

   The other three parts of the marketing mix are product, pricing, and promotion.

a. Job creation programs
b. Matching theory
c. Missing completely at random
d. Distribution

7. The _____ is the labour pool in employment. It is generally used to describe those working for a single company or industry, but can also apply to a geographic region like a city, country, state, etc. The term generally excludes the employers or management, and implies those involved in manual labour.
   a. Workforce
   b. Work-life balance
   c. Division of labour
   d. Pink-collar worker

8. A _____ is a formal statement of a set of business goals, the reasons why they are believed attainable, and the plan for reaching those goals. It may also contain background information about the organization or team attempting to reach those goals.

The business goals may be defined for for-profit or for non-profit organizations.

   a. Distributed management
   b. Crisis management
   c. Business plan
   d. Time management

9. _____, commonly known as e-commerce, consists of the buying and selling of products or services over electronic systems such as the Internet and other computer networks. The amount of trade conducted electronically has grown extraordinarily with widespread Internet usage. The use of commerce is conducted in this way, spurring and drawing on innovations in electronic funds transfer, supply chain management, Internet marketing, online transaction processing, electronic data interchange (EDI), inventory management systems, and automated data collection systems.
   a. Electronic Commerce
   b. A Stake in the Outcome
   c. Online shopping
   d. A4e

10. _____ is one of the four Ps of the marketing mix. The other three aspects are product, promotion, and place. It is also a key variable in microeconomic price allocation theory.
    a. Transfer pricing
    b. Price floor
    c. Penetration pricing
    d. Pricing

11. The _____ is a performance management tool for measuring whether the smaller-scale operational activities of a company are aligned with its larger-scale objectives in terms of vision and strategy.

By focusing not only on financial outcomes but also on the operational, marketing and developmental inputs to these, the _____ helps provide a more comprehensive view of a business, which in turn helps organizations act in their best long-term interests. This tool is also being used to address business response to climate change and greenhouse gas emissions.

   a. Commercial management
   b. Middle management
   c. Balanced scorecard
   d. Management development

12. In decision theory and estimation theory, the _____ of an estimator, $\hat{\theta}$, of an unknown parameter of the distribution, θ, is the expected value of the loss function

$$R(\theta, \hat{\theta}) = \mathbb{E}_\theta L(\theta, \hat{\theta}) = \int L(\theta, \hat{\theta})\, dP_\theta.$$

where dP_θ is a probability measure parametrized by θ.

- For a scalar parameter θ and a quadratic loss function,

$$L(\theta, \hat{\theta}) = (\theta - \hat{\theta})^2$$

the _____ function becomes the mean squared error of the estimate,

$$R(\theta, \hat{\theta}) = E_\theta (\theta - \hat{\theta})^2$$

- In density estimation, the unknown parameter is probability density itself. The loss function is typically chosen to be a norm in an appropriate function space. For example, for L^2 norm,

$$L(f, \hat{f}) = \|f - \hat{f}\|_2^2$$

the _____ function becomes the mean integrated squared error

$$R(f, \hat{f}) = E\|f - \hat{f}\|^2$$

a. Risk aversion
c. Risk
b. Linear model
d. Financial modeling

13. In economics, business, retail, and accounting, a _____ is the value of money that has been used up to produce something, and hence is not available for use anymore. In economics, a _____ is an alternative that is given up as a result of a decision. In business, the _____ may be one of acquisition, in which case the amount of money expended to acquire it is counted as _____.
   a. Cost allocation
   c. Cost
   b. Cost overrun
   d. Fixed costs

14. _____ can be determined as a percentage of gross or net sales derived from use of the asset or a fixed price per unit sold. but there are also other modes and metrics of compensation. A royalty interest is the right to collect a stream of future royalty payments, often used in the oil industry and music industry to describe a percentage ownership of future production or revenues from a given leasehold, which may be divested from the original owner of the asset.
   a. National treatment
   c. Railway Labor Act
   b. Partnership agreement
   d. Royalties

Chapter 6. Franchising and the Entrepreneur

15. _____ is the state or fact of exclusive rights and control over property, which may be an object, land/real estate or intellectual property. An _____ right is also referred to as title. The concept of _____ has existed for thousands of years and in all cultures.
    a. Emanation of the state
    b. A4e
    c. A Stake in the Outcome
    d. Ownership

16. Mystery shopping or Mystery Consumer is a tool used by market research companies to measure quality of retail service or gather specific information about products and services. _____ posing as normal customers perform specific tasks--such as purchasing a product, asking questions, registering complaints or behaving in a certain way - and then provide detailed reports or feedback about their experiences.

    Mystery shopping began in the 1940s as a way to measure employee integrity.

    a. Quantitative marketing research
    b. Questionnaire construction
    c. Questionnaire
    d. Mystery shoppers

17. The _____ of 1936 (or Anti-Price Discrimination Act, 15 U.S.C. § 13) is a United States federal law that prohibits what were considered, at the time of passage, to be anticompetitive practices by producers, specifically price discrimination. It grew out of practices in which chain stores were allowed to purchase goods at lower prices than other retailers.
    a. Privity
    b. Robinson-Patman Act
    c. Labor Management Reporting and Disclosure Act
    d. Bona fide occupational qualification

18. A _____ is a professional who provides advice in a particular area of expertise such as management, accountancy, the environment, entertainment, technology, law , human resources, marketing, medicine, finance, economics, public affairs, communication, engineering, sound system design, graphic design, or waste management.

    A _____ is usually an expert or a professional in a specific field and has a wide knowledge of the subject matter. A _____ usually works for a consultancy firm or is self-employed, and engages with multiple and changing clients.

    a. 33 Strategies of War
    b. Consultant
    c. 1990 Clean Air Act
    d. 28-hour day

19. The _____ is an independent agency of the United States government, established in 1914 by the _____ Act. Its principal mission is the promotion of 'consumer protection' and the elimination and prevention of what regulators perceive to be harmfully 'anti-competitive' business practices, such as coercive monopoly.

    The _____ Act was one of President Wilson's major acts against trusts.

    a. 28-hour day
    b. 1990 Clean Air Act
    c. 33 Strategies of War
    d. Federal Trade Commission

20. A _____ is a business that is privately owned and operated, with a small number of employees and relatively low volume of sales. The legal definition of 'small' often varies by country and industry, but is generally under 100 employees in the United States and under 50 employees in the European Union. In comparison, the definition of mid-sized business by the number of employees is generally under 500 in the U.S. and 250 for the European Union.

Chapter 6. Franchising and the Entrepreneur

   a. Critical Success Factor
   b. Pre-determined overhead rate
   c. Golden Boot Compensation
   d. Small Business

21. The _____ is a United States government agency that provides support to small businesses.

The mission of the _____ is 'to maintain and strengthen the nation's economy by enabling the establishment and viability of small businesses and by assisting in the economic recovery of communities after disasters.'

The _____ makes loans directly to businesses and acts as a guarantor on bank loans. In some circumstances it also makes loans to victims of natural disasters, works to get government procurement contracts for small businesses, and assists businesses with management, technical and training issues.

   a. Small Business Administration
   b. 33 Strategies of War
   c. 1990 Clean Air Act
   d. 28-hour day

22. _____ is an abbreviation for '_____', a legal document used in the franchising process in the United States.

Franchisors must give a _____ to franchisees at least 10 business days before any contract is signed and before any money changes hands. It contains extensive information about a franchisor, which is intended to give potential franchisees enough information to make educated decisions about their investments.

   a. AAAI
   b. A Stake in the Outcome
   c. Uniform Franchise Offering Circular
   d. A4e

23. _____ are legal property rights over creations of the mind, both artistic and commercial, and the corresponding fields of law. Under _____ law, owners are granted certain exclusive rights to a variety of intangible assets, such as musical, literary, and artistic works; ideas, discoveries and inventions; and words, phrases, symbols, and designs. Common types of _____ include copyrights, trademarks, patents, industrial design rights and trade secrets.

   a. Equal Pay Act
   b. Intent
   c. Intellectual property
   d. Unemployment Action Center

24. _____ plant, and equipment, is a term used in accountancy for assets and property which cannot easily be converted into cash. This can be compared with current assets such as cash or bank accounts, which are described as liquid assets. In most cases, only tangible assets are referred to as fixed.

   a. 28-hour day
   b. 33 Strategies of War
   c. 1990 Clean Air Act
   d. Fixed asset

25. Marketing research is a form of business research and is generally divided into two categories: consumer _____ and business-to-business (B2B) _____, which was previously known as industrial marketing research. Consumer marketing research studies the buying habits of individual people while business-to-business marketing research investigates the markets for products sold by one business to another.

Consumer _____ is a form of applied sociology that concentrates on understanding the behaviours, whims and preferences, of consumers in a market-based economy, and aims to understand the effects and comparative success of marketing campaigns.

a. Questionnaire construction
b. Questionnaire
c. Mystery shoppers
d. Market research

26. In finance, an _____ is a contract between a buyer and a seller that gives the buyer the right--but not the obligation--to buy or to sell a particular asset (the underlying asset) at a later day at an agreed price. In return for granting the _____, the seller collects a payment (the premium) from the buyer. A call _____ gives the buyer the right to buy the underlying asset; a put _____ gives the buyer of the _____ the right to sell the underlying asset.
   a. AAAI
   b. A Stake in the Outcome
   c. Option
   d. A4e

27. _____ consists of the mental process of thinking involved with the process of judging the merits of multiple options and selecting one of them for action. Some simple examples include deciding whether to get up in the morning or go back to sleep, or selecting a given route for a journey. More complex examples (often decisions that affect what a person thinks or their core beliefs) include choosing a lifestyle, religious affiliation, or political position.
   a. Choice
   b. Championship mobilization
   c. Groups decision making
   d. Trade study

28. In a human resources context, _____ or labor _____ is the rate at which an employer gains and loses employees. Simple ways to describe it are 'how long employees tend to stay' or 'the rate of traffic through the revolving door.' _____ is measured for individual companies and for their industry as a whole. If an employer is said to have a high _____ relative to its competitors, it means that employees of that company have a shorter average tenure than those of other companies in the same industry.
   a. Continuous
   b. Career portfolios
   c. Ten year occupational employment projection
   d. Turnover

29. _____ or _____ data refers to selected population characteristics as used in government, marketing or opinion research, or the _____ profiles used in such research. Note the distinction from the term 'demography' Commonly-used _____s include race, age, income, disabilities, mobility (in terms of travel time to work or number of vehicles available), educational attainment, home ownership, employment status, and even location.
   a. Adam Smith
   b. Affiliation
   c. Abraham Harold Maslow
   d. Demographic

30. The term '_____' refers to the concept of collecting information and attempting to spot a pattern in the information. In some fields of study, the term '_____' has more formally-defined meanings.

In project management _____ is a mathematical technique that uses historical results to predict future outcome.

   a. Stepwise regression
   b. Regression analysis
   c. Least squares
   d. Trend analysis

31. _____ is an integrated communications-based process through which individuals and communities discover that existing and newly-identified needs and wants may be satisfied by the products and services of others.

Chapter 6. Franchising and the Entrepreneur

_____ is defined by the American _____ Association as the activity, set of institutions, and processes for creating, communicating, delivering, and exchanging offerings that have value for customers, clients, partners, and society at large. The term developed from the original meaning which referred literally to going to market, as in shopping, or going to a market to buy or sell goods or services.

a. Customer relationship management
b. Disruptive technology
c. Market development
d. Marketing

Chapter 7. Buying an Existing Business

1. The _____ is a performance management tool for measuring whether the smaller-scale operational activities of a company are aligned with its larger-scale objectives in terms of vision and strategy.

   By focusing not only on financial outcomes but also on the operational, marketing and developmental inputs to these, the _____ helps provide a more comprehensive view of a business, which in turn helps organizations act in their best long-term interests. This tool is also being used to address business response to climate change and greenhouse gas emissions.

   a. Management development
   b. Middle management
   c. Commercial management
   d. Balanced scorecard

2. _____ is a term used to define maximum possible output of an economy. According to UNCTAD, no agreed-upon definition exists. UNCTAD itself proposes: 'the productive resources, entrepreneurial capabilities and production linkages which together determine the capacity of a country to produce goods and services.' The term '_____' is also used in binary economics to mean income-generating capacity be it of a factory, land, patent or the labour skills of an individual.
   a. Multifactor productivity
   b. Factors of production
   c. Diseconomies of scale
   d. Productive capacity

3. The _____ is the labour pool in employment. It is generally used to describe those working for a single company or industry, but can also apply to a geographic region like a city, country, state, etc. The term generally excludes the employers or management, and implies those involved in manual labour.
   a. Division of labour
   b. Pink-collar worker
   c. Work-life balance
   d. Workforce

4. _____ is the state or fact of exclusive rights and control over property, which may be an object, land/real estate or intellectual property. An _____ right is also referred to as title. The concept of _____ has existed for thousands of years and in all cultures.
   a. Emanation of the state
   b. A4e
   c. A Stake in the Outcome
   d. Ownership

5. In a human resources context, _____ or labor _____ is the rate at which an employer gains and loses employees. Simple ways to describe it are 'how long employees tend to stay' or 'the rate of traffic through the revolving door.' _____ is measured for individual companies and for their industry as a whole. If an employer is said to have a high _____ relative to its competitors, it means that employees of that company have a shorter average tenure than those of other companies in the same industry.
   a. Ten year occupational employment projection
   b. Career portfolios
   c. Continuous
   d. Turnover

6. _____ is Latin for 'Let the buyer beware'. Generally _____ is the property law doctrine that controls the sale of real property after the date of closing.

   Under the doctrine of _____, the buyer could not recover from the seller for defects on the property that rendered the property unfit for ordinary purposes. The only exception was if the seller actively concealed latent defects. The modern trend in the US, however, is one of the Implied Warranty of Fitness that applies only to the sale of new residential housing by a builder-seller and the rule of _____ applies to all other sale situations.

Chapter 7. Buying an Existing Business

a. Caveat emptor
c. 33 Strategies of War
b. 28-hour day
d. 1990 Clean Air Act

7. _____ is one of the four Ps of the marketing mix. The other three aspects are product, promotion, and place. It is also a key variable in microeconomic price allocation theory.

a. Penetration pricing
c. Transfer pricing
b. Price floor
d. Pricing

8. _____ is one of a series of accounting transactions dealing with the billing of customers who owe money to a person, company or organization for goods and services that have been provided to the customer. In most business entities this is typically done by generating an invoice and mailing or electronically delivering it to the customer, who in turn must pay it within an established timeframe called credit or payment terms.

An example of a common payment term is Net 30, meaning payment is due in the amount of the invoice 30 days from the date of invoice.

a. Accounts receivable
c. Accumulated Depreciation
b. Other revenue
d. A Stake in the Outcome

9. _____ is a process and a set of procedures used to estimate the economic value of an owner's interest in a business. Valuation is used by financial market participants to determine the price they are willing to pay or receive to consummate a sale of a business. In addition to estimating the selling price of a business, the same valuation tools are often used by business appraisers to resolve disputes related to estate and gift taxation, divorce litigation, allocate business purchase price among business assets, establish a formula for estimating the value of partners' ownership interest for buy-sell agreements, and many other business and legal purposes.

a. Business valuation
c. Munn v. Illinois
b. Robinson-Patman Act
d. No-FEAR Act

10. _____ refers to the movement of cash into or out of a business or financial product. It is usually measured during a specified, finite period of time. Measurement of _____ can be used

- to determine a project's rate of return or value. The time of _____s into and out of projects are used as inputs in financial models such as internal rate of return, and net present value.
- to determine problems with a business's liquidity. Being profitable does not necessarily mean being liquid. A company can fail because of a shortage of cash, even while profitable.
- as an alternate measure of a business's profits when it is believed that accrual accounting concepts do not represent economic realities. For example, a company may be notionally profitable but generating little operational cash (as may be the case for a company that barters its products rather than selling for cash.) In such a case, the company may be deriving additional operating cash by issuing shares evaluating default risk, re-investment requirements, etc.

_____ is a generic term used differently depending on the context. It may be defined by users for their own purposes.

a. Gross profit
c. Gross profit margin
b. Sweat equity
d. Cash flow

Chapter 7. Buying an Existing Business

11. _____ is a file or account that contains money that a person or company owes to suppliers, but has not paid yet (a form of debt.) When you receive an invoice you add it to the file, and then you remove it when you pay. Thus, the A/P is a form of credit that suppliers offer to their purchasers by allowing them to pay for a product or service after it has already been received.
    a. Accounts receivable
    b. A Stake in the Outcome
    c. Other revenue
    d. Accounts payable

12. The phrase mergers and _____s refers to the aspect of corporate strategy, corporate finance and management dealing with the buying, selling and combining of different companies that can aid, finance, or help a growing company in a given industry grow rapidly without having to create another business entity.

    An _____, also known as a takeover or a buyout, is the buying of one company (the 'target') by another. An _____ may be friendly or hostile.

    a. A4e
    b. Acquisition
    c. AAAI
    d. A Stake in the Outcome

13. _____ is the set of tasks, knowledge, and techniques required to identify business needs and determine solutions to business problems. Solutions often include a systems development component, but may also consist of process improvement or organizational change. The person who carries out this task is called a business analyst or _____.
    a. Door-to-door selling
    b. 1990 Clean Air Act
    c. 28-hour day
    d. Business analysis

14. _____ consists of the mental process of thinking involved with the process of judging the merits of multiple options and selecting one of them for action. Some simple examples include deciding whether to get up in the morning or go back to sleep, or selecting a given route for a journey. More complex examples (often decisions that affect what a person thinks or their core beliefs) include choosing a lifestyle, religious affiliation, or political position.
    a. Groups decision making
    b. Championship mobilization
    c. Trade study
    d. Choice

15. In finance, an _____ is a contract between a buyer and a seller that gives the buyer the right--but not the obligation--to buy or to sell a particular asset (the underlying asset) at a later day at an agreed price. In return for granting the _____, the seller collects a payment (the premium) from the buyer. A call _____ gives the buyer the right to buy the underlying asset; a put _____ gives the buyer of the _____ the right to sell the underlying asset.
    a. A Stake in the Outcome
    b. Option
    c. AAAI
    d. A4e

16. A _____ is a professional who provides advice in a particular area of expertise such as management, accountancy, the environment, entertainment, technology, law , human resources, marketing, medicine, finance, economics, public affairs, communication, engineering, sound system design, graphic design, or waste management.

    A _____ is usually an expert or a professional in a specific field and has a wide knowledge of the subject matter. A _____ usually works for a consultancy firm or is self-employed, and engages with multiple and changing clients.

Chapter 7. Buying an Existing Business

a. 33 Strategies of War
b. 1990 Clean Air Act
c. 28-hour day
d. Consultant

17. _____ is a term used for a number of concepts involving either the performance of an investigation of a business or person, or the performance of an act with a certain standard of care. It can be a legal obligation, but the term will more commonly apply to voluntary investigations. A common example of _____ in various industries is the process through which a potential acquirer evaluates a target company or its assets for acquisition.

a. Technology transfer
b. Flextime
c. Negligence in employment
d. Due diligence

18. In decision theory and estimation theory, the _____ of an estimator, $\hat{\theta}$, of an unknown parameter of the distribution, θ, is the expected value of the loss function

$$R(\theta, \hat{\theta}) = \mathbb{E}_\theta L(\theta, \hat{\theta}) = \int L(\theta, \hat{\theta})\, dP_\theta.$$

where dP_θ is a probability measure parametrized by θ.

- For a scalar parameter θ and a quadratic loss function,

$$L(\theta, \hat{\theta}) = (\theta - \hat{\theta})^2$$

the _____ function becomes the mean squared error of the estimate,

$$R(\theta, \hat{\theta}) = E_\theta (\theta - \hat{\theta})^2$$

- In density estimation, the unknown parameter is probability density itself. The loss function is typically chosen to be a norm in an appropriate function space. For example, for L^2 norm,

$$L(f, \hat{f}) = \|f - \hat{f}\|_2^2$$

the _____ function becomes the mean integrated squared error

$$R(f, \hat{f}) = E\|f - \hat{f}\|^2$$

a. Risk
b. Linear model
c. Financial modeling
d. Risk aversion

Chapter 7. Buying an Existing Business

19. _____ according to Onuoha (2007) is the practice of starting new organizations or revitalizing mature organizations, particularly new businesses generally in response to identified opportunities. _____ is often a difficult undertaking, as a vast majority of new businesses fail. Entrepreneurial activities are substantially different depending on the type of organization that is being started.

   a. A4e
   b. A Stake in the Outcome
   c. AAAI
   d. Entrepreneurship

20. In business and accounting, _____s are everything of value that is owned by a person or company. Any property or object of value that one possesses, usually considered as applicable to the payment of one's debts is considered an _____. Simplistically stated, _____s are things of value that can be readily converted into cash.

   a. AAAI
   b. Asset
   c. A4e
   d. A Stake in the Outcome

21. _____ are formal records of the financial activities of a business, person, or other entity. In British English, including United Kingdom company law, _____ are often referred to as accounts, although the term _____ is also used, particularly by accountants.

   _____ provide an overview of a business or person's financial condition in both short and long term.

   a. 28-hour day
   b. 33 Strategies of War
   c. Financial statements
   d. 1990 Clean Air Act

22. _____ are defined as identifiable non-monetary assets that cannot be seen, touched or physically measured, which are created through time and/or effort and that are identifiable as a separate asset. There are two primary forms of intangibles - legal intangibles (such as trade secrets (e.g., customer lists), copyrights, patents, trademarks, and goodwill) and competitive intangibles (such as knowledge activities (know-how, knowledge), collaboration activities, leverage activities, and structural activities.) Legal intangibles are known under the generic term intellectual property and generate legal property rights defensible in a court of law.

   a. Interlocking directorate
   b. Induction programme
   c. Employee value proposition
   d. Intangible assets

23. _____ is the price at which an asset would trade in a competitive Walrasian auction setting. _____ is often used interchangeably with open _____, fair value or fair _____, although these terms have distinct definitions in different standards, and may differ in some circumstances.

   International Valuation Standards defines _____ as 'the estimated amount for which a property should exchange on the date of valuation between a willing buyer and a willing seller in an arm's-length transaction after proper marketing wherein the parties had each acted knowledgeably, prudently, and without compulsion.'

   _____ is a concept distinct from market price, which is 'the price at which one can transact', while _____ is 'the true underlying value' according to theoretical standards.

   a. Restructuring
   b. Payback period
   c. Market value added
   d. Market value

Chapter 7. Buying an Existing Business

24. _____ is a form of communication that typically attempts to persuade potential customers to purchase or to consume more of a particular brand of product or service. 'While now central to the contemporary global economy and the reproduction of global production networks, it is only quite recently that _____ has been more than a marginal influence on patterns of sales and production. The formation of modern _____ was intimately bound up with the emergence of new forms of monopoly capitalism around the end of the 19th and beginning of the 20th century as one element in corporate strategies to create, organize and where possible control markets, especially for mass produced consumer goods.
   a. Advertising
   b. AAAI
   c. A Stake in the Outcome
   d. A4e

25. _____ are legal property rights over creations of the mind, both artistic and commercial, and the corresponding fields of law. Under _____ law, owners are granted certain exclusive rights to a variety of intangible assets, such as musical, literary, and artistic works; ideas, discoveries and inventions; and words, phrases, symbols, and designs. Common types of _____ include copyrights, trademarks, patents, industrial design rights and trade secrets.
   a. Unemployment Action Center
   b. Equal Pay Act
   c. Intent
   d. Intellectual property

26. _____ generally refers to a list of all planned expenses and revenues. It is a plan for saving and spending. A _____ is an important concept in microeconomics, which uses a _____ line to illustrate the trade-offs between two or more goods.
   a. 28-hour day
   b. 33 Strategies of War
   c. 1990 Clean Air Act
   d. Budget

27. _____, commonly known as e-commerce, consists of the buying and selling of products or services over electronic systems such as the Internet and other computer networks. The amount of trade conducted electronically has grown extraordinarily with widespread Internet usage. The use of commerce is conducted in this way, spurring and drawing on innovations in electronic funds transfer, supply chain management, Internet marketing, online transaction processing, electronic data interchange (EDI), inventory management systems, and automated data collection systems.
   a. A Stake in the Outcome
   b. A4e
   c. Online shopping
   d. Electronic Commerce

28. _____ plant, and equipment, is a term used in accountancy for assets and property which cannot easily be converted into cash. This can be compared with current assets such as cash or bank accounts, which are described as liquid assets. In most cases, only tangible assets are referred to as fixed.
   a. 33 Strategies of War
   b. 28-hour day
   c. 1990 Clean Air Act
   d. Fixed asset

29. An _____, or organogram(me)) is a diagram that shows the structure of an organization and the relationships and relative ranks of its parts and positions/jobs. The term is also used for similar diagrams, for example ones showing the different elements of a field of knowledge or a group of languages. The French Encyclopédie had one of the first _____s of knowledge in general.
   a. AAAI
   b. A4e
   c. A Stake in the Outcome
   d. Organizational chart

30. A _____ is a formal statement of a set of business goals, the reasons why they are believed attainable, and the plan for reaching those goals. It may also contain background information about the organization or team attempting to reach those goals.

Chapter 7. Buying an Existing Business

The business goals may be defined for for-profit or for non-profit organizations.

a. Time management
b. Distributed management
c. Crisis management
d. Business plan

31. _____ in marketing and strategic management is an assessment of the strengths and weaknesses of current and potential competitors. This analysis provides both an offensive and defensive strategic context through which to identify opportunities and threats. Competitor profiling coalesces all of the relevant sources of _____ into one framework in the support of efficient and effective strategy formulation, implementation, monitoring and adjustment.

a. Competitor or Competitive Intelligence
b. Competitor analysis
c. 28-hour day
d. 1990 Clean Air Act

32. _____ is an advertisement in which a particular product specifically mentions a competitor by name for the express purpose of showing why the competitor is inferior to the product naming it.

This should not be confused with parody advertisements, where a fictional product is being advertised for the purpose of poking fun at the particular advertisement, nor should it be confused with the use of a coined brand name for the purpose of comparing the product without actually naming an actual competitor. ('Wikipedia tastes better and is less filling than the Encyclopedia Galactica.')

In the 1980s, during what has been referred to as the cola wars, soft-drink manufacturer Pepsi ran a series of advertisements where people, caught on hidden camera, in a blind taste test, chose Pepsi over rival Coca-Cola.

a. Comparative advertising
b. 1990 Clean Air Act
c. 33 Strategies of War
d. 28-hour day

33. Title _____s serve as guarantees to the recipient of property, ensuring that the recipient receives what he or she bargained for. The English _____s of title, sometimes included in deeds to real property, are that the grantor is lawfully seized (in fee simple) of the property, (2) that the grantor has the right to convey the property to the grantee, (3) that the property is conveyed without encumbrances (this _____ is frequently modified to allow for certain encumbrances), (4) that the grantor has done no act to encumber the property, (5) that the grantee shall have quiet possession of the property, and (6) that the grantor will execute such further assurances of the land as may be requisite (Nos. 3 and 4, which overlap significantly, are sometimes treated as one item.)

a. Trade secret
b. Business valuation
c. Covenant
d. Hostile work environment

34. A _____ or covenant not to compete, is a term used in contract law under which one party (usually an employee) agrees to not pursue a similar profession or trade in competition against another party (usually the employer.) As a contract provision, a _____ is bound by traditional contract requirements including the consideration doctrine. The use of such clauses is premised on the possibility that upon their termination or resignation, an employee might begin working for a competitor or starting a business, and gain competitive advantage by abusing confidential information about their former employer's operations or trade secrets, or sensitive information such as customer/client lists, business practices, upcoming products, and marketing plans.

Chapter 7. Buying an Existing Business

a. Postcautionary principle
b. Trade secret
c. Non-compete clause
d. Contrat nouvelle embauche

35. A _____ is a clause in a loan or promissory note that stipulates that the full balance may be called due upon sale or transfer of ownership of the property used to secure the note. The lender has the right, but not the obligation, to call the note due in such a circumstance.

Virtually all recent mortgages made in the United States contain a _____.

a. 28-hour day
b. Joint and several liability
c. Due-on-sale clause
d. 1990 Clean Air Act

36. _____ is the area of law in which manufacturers, distributors, suppliers, retailers, and others who make products available to the public are held responsible for the injuries those products cause.

In the United States, the claims most commonly associated with _____ are negligence, strict liability, breach of warranty, and various consumer protection claims. The majority of _____ laws are determined at the state level and vary widely from state to state.

a. Leave of absence
b. Right-to-work laws
c. Railway Labor Act
d. Product liability

37. _____ , also referred to simply as a 'public offering' or 'flotation,' is when a company issues common stock or shares to the public for the first time. They are often issued by smaller, younger companies seeking capital to expand, but can also be done by large privately-owned companies looking to become publicly traded.

In an _____ the issuer may obtain the assistance of an underwriting firm, which helps it determine what type of security to issue (common or preferred), best offering price and time to bring it to market.

a. Occupational Safety and Health Administration
b. Unemployment insurance
c. Outsourcing
d. Initial public offering

38. In financial accounting, a _____ or statement of financial position is a summary of a person's or organization's balances. Assets, liabilities and ownership equity are listed as of a specific date, such as the end of its financial year. A _____ is often described as a snapshot of a company's financial condition.

a. 1990 Clean Air Act
b. 33 Strategies of War
c. Balance sheet
d. 28-hour day

39. In business, _____ is the total liabilities minus total outside assets of an individual or a company. For a company, this is called shareholders' preference and may be referred to as book value. _____ is stated as at a particular year in time.

a. Net worth
b. Payback period
c. Novated lease
d. Deferred compensation

Chapter 7. Buying an Existing Business

40. _____ or economic opportunity loss is the value of the next best alternative forgone as the result of making a decision. _____ analysis is an important part of a company's decision-making processes but is not treated as an actual cost in any financial statement. The next best thing that a person can engage in is referred to as the _____ of doing the best thing and ignoring the next best thing to be done.
   a. A4e
   b. AAAI
   c. A Stake in the Outcome
   d. Opportunity cost

41. In economics, business, retail, and accounting, a _____ is the value of money that has been used up to produce something, and hence is not available for use anymore. In economics, a _____ is an alternative that is given up as a result of a decision. In business, the _____ may be one of acquisition, in which case the amount of money expended to acquire it is counted as _____.
   a. Cost overrun
   b. Fixed costs
   c. Cost allocation
   d. Cost

42. A _____ is a corporation in the United States that, for Federal income tax purposes, is taxed under 26 U.S.C. Â§ 11 and Subchapter C (26 U.S.C.
   a. 1990 Clean Air Act
   b. C corporation
   c. 33 Strategies of War
   d. 28-hour day

43. An _____, for United States federal income tax purposes, is a corporation that makes a valid election to be taxed under Subchapter S of Chapter 1 of the Internal Revenue Code.

    In general, _____s do not pay any income taxes. Instead, the corporation's income or losses are divided among and passed through to its shareholders.

   a. 33 Strategies of War
   b. 28-hour day
   c. 1990 Clean Air Act
   d. S corporation

44. A _____ is a type of business entity in which partners (owners) share with each other the profits or losses of the business. _____s are often favored over corporations for taxation purposes, as the _____ structure does not generally incur a tax on profits before it is distributed to the partners (i.e. there is no dividend tax levied.) However, depending on the _____ structure and the jurisdiction in which it operates, owners of a _____ may be exposed to greater personal liability than they would as shareholders of a corporation.
   a. Partnership
   b. Federal Employers Liability Act
   c. Due process
   d. Mediation

45. A _____ is a form of partnership similar to a general partnership, except that in addition to one or more general partners (GPs), there are one or more limited partners (_____s.) It is a partnership in which only one partner is required to be a general partner.

    The GPs are, in all major respects, in the same legal position as partners in a conventional firm, i.e. they have management control, share the right to use partnership property, share the profits of the firm in predefined proportions, and have joint and several liability for the debts of the partnership.

a. Private equity
b. Limited partnership
c. Pension fund
d. Growth capital

46. _____ is the corporate management term for the act of reorganizing the legal, ownership, operational, or other structures of a company for the purpose of making it more profitable, or better organized for its present needs. Alternate reasons for _____ include a change of ownership or ownership structure, demerger repositioning debt _____ and financial _____.
a. Net worth
b. Market value
c. Restructuring
d. Market value added

47. _____, or Value optimized pricing is a business strategy. It sets selling prices on the perceived value to the customer, rather than on the actual cost of the product, the market price, competitors prices, or the historical price.

The goal of value-based pricing is to align price with value delivered.

a. Centralization
b. Supervisory board
c. Chief legal officer
d. Value based pricing

Chapter 8. Building a Powerful Marketing Plan

1. _____ is an integrated communications-based process through which individuals and communities discover that existing and newly-identified needs and wants may be satisfied by the products and services of others.

   _____ is defined by the American _____ Association as the activity, set of institutions, and processes for creating, communicating, delivering, and exchanging offerings that have value for customers, clients, partners, and society at large. The term developed from the original meaning which referred literally to going to market, as in shopping, or going to a market to buy or sell goods or services.

   a. Disruptive technology
   c. Market development
   b. Marketing
   d. Customer relationship management

2. A _____ is a written document that details the necessary actions to achieve one or more marketing objectives. It can be for a product or service, a brand, or a product line. _____s cover between one and five years.
   a. Marketing strategy
   c. Disruptive technology
   b. Market development
   d. Marketing plan

3. A _____ is a formal statement of a set of business goals, the reasons why they are believed attainable, and the plan for reaching those goals. It may also contain background information about the organization or team attempting to reach those goals.

   The business goals may be defined for for-profit or for non-profit organizations.

   a. Crisis management
   c. Time management
   b. Distributed management
   d. Business plan

4. _____ is an unconventional system of promotions that relies on time, energy and imagination rather than a big marketing budget. Typically, _____ tactics are unexpected and unconventional; consumers are targeted in unexpected places, which can make the idea that's being marketed memorable, generate buzz, and even spread virally. The term was coined and defined by Jay Conrad Levinson in his 1984 book _____.
   a. Guerrilla marketing
   c. 28-hour day
   b. Relationship marketing
   d. 1990 Clean Air Act

5. The phrase mergers and _____s refers to the aspect of corporate strategy, corporate finance and management dealing with the buying, selling and combining of different companies that can aid, finance, or help a growing company in a given industry grow rapidly without having to create another business entity.

   An _____, also known as a takeover or a buyout, is the buying of one company (the 'target') by another. An _____ may be friendly or hostile.

   a. AAAI
   c. A Stake in the Outcome
   b. A4e
   d. Acquisition

6. _____, commonly known as e-commerce, consists of the buying and selling of products or services over electronic systems such as the Internet and other computer networks. The amount of trade conducted electronically has grown extraordinarily with widespread Internet usage. The use of commerce is conducted in this way, spurring and drawing on innovations in electronic funds transfer, supply chain management, Internet marketing, online transaction processing, electronic data interchange (EDI), inventory management systems, and automated data collection systems.

a. A Stake in the Outcome
b. Online shopping
c. A4e
d. Electronic Commerce

7. _____ is a form of communication that typically attempts to persuade potential customers to purchase or to consume more of a particular brand of product or service. 'While now central to the contemporary global economy and the reproduction of global production networks, it is only quite recently that _____ has been more than a marginal influence on patterns of sales and production. The formation of modern _____ was intimately bound up with the emergence of new forms of monopoly capitalism around the end of the 19th and beginning of the 20th century as one element in corporate strategies to create, organize and where possible control markets, especially for mass produced consumer goods.

a. AAAI
b. A4e
c. A Stake in the Outcome
d. Advertising

8. The 'business case for _____', theorizes that in a global marketplace, a company that employs a diverse workforce (both men and women, people of many generations, people from ethnically and racially diverse backgrounds etc.) is better able to understand the demographics of the marketplace it serves and is thus better equipped to thrive in that marketplace than a company that has a more limited range of employee demographics.

An additional corollary suggests that a company that supports the _____ of its workforce can also improve employee satisfaction, productivity and retention.

a. Trademark
b. Diversity
c. Kanban
d. Virtual team

9. _____ is the provision of service to customers before, during and after a purchase.

According to Turban et al. (2002), '_____ is a series of activities designed to enhance the level of customer satisfaction - that is, the feeling that a product or service has met the customer expectation.'

Its importance varies by product, industry and customer; defective or broken merchandise can be exchanged, often only with a receipt and within a specified time frame.

a. Service rate
b. Customer service
c. 28-hour day
d. 1990 Clean Air Act

10. _____ is the state or fact of exclusive rights and control over property, which may be an object, land/real estate or intellectual property. An _____ right is also referred to as title. The concept of _____ has existed for thousands of years and in all cultures.

a. A Stake in the Outcome
b. Ownership
c. Emanation of the state
d. A4e

11. _____ is an advertisement in which a particular product specifically mentions a competitor by name for the express purpose of showing why the competitor is inferior to the product naming it.

Chapter 8. Building a Powerful Marketing Plan

This should not be confused with parody advertisements, where a fictional product is being advertised for the purpose of poking fun at the particular advertisement, nor should it be confused with the use of a coined brand name for the purpose of comparing the product without actually naming an actual competitor. ('Wikipedia tastes better and is less filling than the Encyclopedia Galactica.')

In the 1980s, during what has been referred to as the cola wars, soft-drink manufacturer Pepsi ran a series of advertisements where people, caught on hidden camera, in a blind taste test, chose Pepsi over rival Coca-Cola.

a. 33 Strategies of War
b. 1990 Clean Air Act
c. 28-hour day
d. Comparative advertising

12. _____ or _____ data refers to selected population characteristics as used in government, marketing or opinion research, or the _____ profiles used in such research. Note the distinction from the term 'demography' Commonly-used _____s include race, age, income, disabilities, mobility (in terms of travel time to work or number of vehicles available), educational attainment, home ownership, employment status, and even location.

a. Demographic
b. Abraham Harold Maslow
c. Affiliation
d. Adam Smith

13. Marketing research is a form of business research and is generally divided into two categories: consumer _____ and business-to-business (B2B) _____, which was previously known as industrial marketing research. Consumer marketing research studies the buying habits of individual people while business-to-business marketing research investigates the markets for products sold by one business to another.

Consumer _____ is a form of applied sociology that concentrates on understanding the behaviours, whims and preferences, of consumers in a market-based economy, and aims to understand the effects and comparative success of marketing campaigns.

a. Mystery shoppers
b. Questionnaire construction
c. Questionnaire
d. Market research

14. _____, commonly abbreviated to Gen X, is a term used to refer to a generational cohort of children born after the baby boom ended and usually prior to the 1980s

The term _____ has been used in demography, the social sciences, and marketing, though it is most often used in popular culture.

In the U.S. _____ was originally referred to as the 'baby bust' generation because of the drop in the birth rate following the baby boom.

a. Affiliation
b. Abraham Harold Maslow
c. Adam Smith
d. Generation X

15. _____ is a term used for a number of concepts involving either the performance of an investigation of a business or person, or the performance of an act with a certain standard of care. It can be a legal obligation, but the term will more commonly apply to voluntary investigations. A common example of _____ in various industries is the process through which a potential acquirer evaluates a target company or its assets for acquisition.
   a. Technology transfer
   b. Negligence in employment
   c. Flextime
   d. Due diligence

16. The term '_____' refers to the concept of collecting information and attempting to spot a pattern in the information. In some fields of study, the term '_____' has more formally-defined meanings.

In project management _____ is a mathematical technique that uses historical results to predict future outcome.

   a. Trend analysis
   b. Stepwise regression
   c. Least squares
   d. Regression analysis

17. A _____ is a form of qualitative research in which a group of people are asked about their attitude towards a product, service, concept, advertisement, idea, or packaging. Questions are asked in an interactive group setting where participants are free to talk with other group members.

The first _____s were created at the Bureau of Applied Social Research by associate director, sociologist Robert K. Merton.

   a. Marketing research
   b. 1990 Clean Air Act
   c. Market analysis
   d. Focus group

18. _____ is the process of estimation in unknown situations. Prediction is a similar, but more general term. Both can refer to estimation of time series, cross-sectional or longitudinal data.
   a. Forecasting
   b. 33 Strategies of War
   c. 28-hour day
   d. 1990 Clean Air Act

19. A _____ is a research instrument consisting of a series of questions and other prompts for the purpose of gathering information from respondents. Although they are often designed for statistical analysis of the responses, this is not always the case. The _____ was invented by Sir Francis Galton.
   a. Questionnaire construction
   b. Structured interview
   c. Questionnaire
   d. Mystery shoppers

20. The _____ is a performance management tool for measuring whether the smaller-scale operational activities of a company are aligned with its larger-scale objectives in terms of vision and strategy.

By focusing not only on financial outcomes but also on the operational, marketing and developmental inputs to these, the _____ helps provide a more comprehensive view of a business, which in turn helps organizations act in their best long-term interests. This tool is also being used to address business response to climate change and greenhouse gas emissions.

Chapter 8. Building a Powerful Marketing Plan

a. Middle management
b. Management development
c. Commercial management
d. Balanced scorecard

21. _____ refers to the movement of cash into or out of a business or financial product. It is usually measured during a specified, finite period of time. Measurement of _____ can be used

- to determine a project's rate of return or value. The time of _____s into and out of projects are used as inputs in financial models such as internal rate of return, and net present value.
- to determine problems with a business's liquidity. Being profitable does not necessarily mean being liquid. A company can fail because of a shortage of cash, even while profitable.
- as an alternate measure of a business's profits when it is believed that accrual accounting concepts do not represent economic realities. For example, a company may be notionally profitable but generating little operational cash (as may be the case for a company that barters its products rather than selling for cash.) In such a case, the company may be deriving additional operating cash by issuing shares evaluating default risk, re-investment requirements, etc.

_____ is a generic term used differently depending on the context. It may be defined by users for their own purposes.

a. Sweat equity
b. Cash flow
c. Gross profit margin
d. Gross profit

22. _____ is the process of extracting hidden patterns from data. As more data is gathered, with the amount of data doubling every three years, _____ is becoming an increasingly important tool to transform this data into information. It is commonly used in a wide range of profiling practices, such as marketing, surveillance, fraud detection and scientific discovery.

a. Decision tree learning
b. Data mining
c. 28-hour day
d. 1990 Clean Air Act

23. _____ consists of the mental process of thinking involved with the process of judging the merits of multiple options and selecting one of them for action. Some simple examples include deciding whether to get up in the morning or go back to sleep, or selecting a given route for a journey. More complex examples (often decisions that affect what a person thinks or their core beliefs) include choosing a lifestyle, religious affiliation, or political position.

a. Trade study
b. Choice
c. Groups decision making
d. Championship mobilization

24. A _____ is a professional who provides advice in a particular area of expertise such as management, accountancy, the environment, entertainment, technology, law , human resources, marketing, medicine, finance, economics, public affairs, communication, engineering, sound system design, graphic design, or waste management.

A _____ is usually an expert or a professional in a specific field and has a wide knowledge of the subject matter. A _____ usually works for a consultancy firm or is self-employed, and engages with multiple and changing clients.

a. Consultant
b. 1990 Clean Air Act
c. 33 Strategies of War
d. 28-hour day

Chapter 8. Building a Powerful Marketing Plan

25. _____ consists of the processes a company uses to track and organize its contacts with its current and prospective customers. _____ software is used to support these processes; information about customers and customer interactions can be entered, stored and accessed by employees in different company departments. Typical _____ goals are to improve services provided to customers, and to use customer contact information for targeted marketing.

   a. Disruptive technology
   b. Green marketing
   c. Marketing plan
   d. Customer relationship management

26. _____ is a form of marketing developed from direct response marketing campaigns conducted in the 1970s and 1980s which emphasizes customer retention and satisfaction, rather than a dominant focus on point-of-sale transactions.

   _____ differs from other forms of marketing in that it recognizes the long term value to the firm of keeping customers, as opposed to direct or 'Intrusion' marketing, which focuses upon acquisition of new clients by targeting majority demographics based upon prospective client lists.

   _____ refers to a long-term and mutually beneficial arrangement wherein both the buyer and seller focus on value enhancement with the goal of providing a more satisfying exchange.

   a. Guerrilla marketing
   b. 1990 Clean Air Act
   c. Relationship marketing
   d. 28-hour day

27. _____ is, in very basic words, a position a firm occupies against its competitors.

   According to Michael Porter, the three methods for creating a sustainable _____ are through:

   1. Cost leadership

   2. Differentiation

   3. Focus (economics)

   a. Theory Z
   b. 1990 Clean Air Act
   c. 28-hour day
   d. Competitive advantage

28. In decision theory and estimation theory, the _____ of an estimator, $\hat{\theta}$, of an unknown parameter of the distribution, θ, is the expected value of the loss function

$$R(\theta, \hat{\theta}) = \mathbb{E}_\theta L(\theta, \hat{\theta}) = \int L(\theta, \hat{\theta})\, dP_\theta.$$

Chapter 8. Building a Powerful Marketing Plan

where dP_θ is a probability measure parametrized by θ.

- For a scalar parameter θ and a quadratic loss function,

$$L(\theta, \hat{\theta}) = (\theta - \hat{\theta})^2$$

the _____ function becomes the mean squared error of the estimate,

$$R(\theta, \hat{\theta}) = E_\theta (\theta - \hat{\theta})^2$$

- In density estimation, the unknown parameter is probability density itself. The loss function is typically chosen to be a norm in an appropriate function space. For example, for L^2 norm,

$$L(f, \hat{f}) = \|f - \hat{f}\|_2^2$$

the _____ function becomes the mean integrated squared error

$$R(f, \hat{f}) = E\|f - \hat{f}\|^2$$

a. Linear model
c. Financial modeling
b. Risk
d. Risk aversion

29. The _____ is a marketing concept that was first proposed as a theory to explain a pattern among successful advertising campaigns of the early 1940s. It states that such campaigns made unique propositions to the customer and that this convinced them to switch brands. The term was invented by Rosser Reeves of Ted Bates ' Company.

a. AAAI
c. A4e
b. A Stake in the Outcome
d. Unique selling proposition

30. _____ is the sum of all experiences a customer has with a supplier of goods or services, over the duration of their relationship with that supplier. It can also be used to mean an individual experience over one transaction; the distinction is usually clear in context.

Analysts and commentators who write about _____ and CRM have increasingly recognized the importance of managing the customer's experience.

a. Customer experience
c. Customer service
b. 1990 Clean Air Act
d. 28-hour day

31. In economics, business, retail, and accounting, a _____ is the value of money that has been used up to produce something, and hence is not available for use anymore. In economics, a _____ is an alternative that is given up as a result of a decision. In business, the _____ may be one of acquisition, in which case the amount of money expended to acquire it is counted as _____.
   a. Cost overrun
   b. Fixed costs
   c. Cost allocation
   d. Cost

32. The concept of quality costs is a means to quantify the total _____-related efforts and deficiencies. It was first described by Armand V. Feigenbaum in a 1956 Harvard Business Review article.

Prior to its introduction, the general perception was that higher quality requires higher costs, either by buying better materials or machines or by hiring more labor.

   a. Cost accounting
   b. Quality costs
   c. Fixed costs
   d. Cost of quality

33. In probability theory, a probability distribution is called _____ if its cumulative distribution function is _____. This is equivalent to saying that for random variables X with the distribution in question, Pr[X = a] = 0 for all real numbers a, i.e.: the probability that X attains the value a is zero, for any number a. If the distribution of X is _____ then X is called a _____ random variable.
   a. Continuous
   b. Decision tree pruning
   c. Connectionist expert systems
   d. Pay Band

34. _____ is a management process whereby delivery (customer valued) processes are constantly evaluated and improved in the light of their efficiency, effectiveness and flexibility.

Some see it as a meta process for most management systems (Business Process Management, Quality Management, Project Management). Deming saw it as part of the 'system' whereby feedback from the process and customer were evaluated against organisational goals.

   a. First-mover advantage
   b. Critical Success Factor
   c. Sole proprietorship
   d. Continuous Improvement Process

35. _____ is a business management strategy aimed at embedding awareness of quality in all organizational processes. _____ has been widely used in manufacturing, education, hospitals, call centers, government, and service industries, as well as NASA space and science programs.

As defined by the International Organization for Standardization (ISO):

> '_____ is a management approach for an organization, centered on quality, based on the participation of all its members and aiming at long-term success through customer satisfaction, and benefits to all members of the organization and to society.' ISO 8402:1994

One major aim is to reduce variation from every process so that greater consistency of effort is obtained. (Royse, D., Thyer, B., Padgett D., ' Logan T., 2006)

a. 1990 Clean Air Act
b. 28-hour day
c. Quality management
d. Total quality management

36. _____ can be considered to have three main components: quality control, quality assurance and quality improvement. _____ is focused not only on product quality, but also the means to achieve it. _____ therefore uses quality assurance and control of processes as well as products to achieve more consistent quality.
a. Total quality management
b. Quality management
c. 28-hour day
d. 1990 Clean Air Act

37. _____, a business term, is a measure of how products and services supplied by a company meet or surpass customer expectation. It is seen as a key performance indicator within business and is part of the four perspectives of a Balanced Scorecard.

In a competitive marketplace where businesses compete for customers, _____ is seen as a key differentiator and increasingly has become a key element of business strategy.

a. Critical Success Factor
b. Customer satisfaction
c. Foreign ownership
d. Horizontal integration

38. The _____ is the labour pool in employment. It is generally used to describe those working for a single company or industry, but can also apply to a geographic region like a city, country, state, etc. The term generally excludes the employers or management, and implies those involved in manual labour.
a. Pink-collar worker
b. Work-life balance
c. Division of labour
d. Workforce

39. _____ is one of the four elements of marketing mix. An organization or set of organizations (go-betweens) involved in the process of making a product or service available for use or consumption by a consumer or business user.

The other three parts of the marketing mix are product, pricing, and promotion.

a. Job creation programs
b. Missing completely at random
c. Matching theory
d. Distribution

40. The _____ is generally accepted as the use and specification of the 'four P's' describing the strategic position of a product in the marketplace. One version of the _____ originated in 1948 when James Culliton said that a marketing decision should be a result of something similar to a recipe. This version was used in 1953 when Neil Borden, in his American Marketing Association presidential address, took the recipe idea one step further and coined the term 'marketing-mix'.
a. 28-hour day
b. 1990 Clean Air Act
c. Marketing mix
d. 33 Strategies of War

41. _____ is one of the four Ps of the marketing mix. The other three aspects are product, promotion, and place. It is also a key variable in microeconomic price allocation theory.
a. Price floor
b. Transfer pricing
c. Penetration pricing
d. Pricing

Chapter 8. Building a Powerful Marketing Plan

42. _____ Management is the succession of strategies used by management as a product goes through its _____. The conditions in which a product is sold changes over time and must be managed as it moves through its succession of stages.

The _____ goes through many phases, involves many professional disciplines, and requires many skills, tools and processes.

- a. Strategic Alliance
- b. Job hunting
- c. Golden handshake
- d. Product life cycle

43. _____ is a marketing strategy 'in which one firm tries to distinguish its product or service from competing products on the basis of attributes like design and workmanship' (McConnell-Brue, 2002, p. 437-438). The firm can also distinguish its product offering through quality of service, extensive distribution, customer focus, or any other sustainable competitive advantage other than price. It can be contrasted with price competition, which is where a company tries to distinguish its product or service from competing products on the basis of low price.

- a. 28-hour day
- b. Non-price competition
- c. 1990 Clean Air Act
- d. 33 Strategies of War

Chapter 9. E-Commerce and the Entrepreneur

1. _____, commonly known as e-commerce, consists of the buying and selling of products or services over electronic systems such as the Internet and other computer networks. The amount of trade conducted electronically has grown extraordinarily with widespread Internet usage. The use of commerce is conducted in this way, spurring and drawing on innovations in electronic funds transfer, supply chain management, Internet marketing, online transaction processing, electronic data interchange (EDI), inventory management systems, and automated data collection systems.

   a. A Stake in the Outcome
   b. A4e
   c. Online shopping
   d. Electronic Commerce

2. _____ is a form of communication that typically attempts to persuade potential customers to purchase or to consume more of a particular brand of product or service. 'While now central to the contemporary global economy and the reproduction of global production networks, it is only quite recently that _____ has been more than a marginal influence on patterns of sales and production. The formation of modern _____ was intimately bound up with the emergence of new forms of monopoly capitalism around the end of the 19th and beginning of the 20th century as one element in corporate strategies to create, organize and where possible control markets, especially for mass produced consumer goods.

   a. A4e
   b. AAAI
   c. Advertising
   d. A Stake in the Outcome

3. _____ consists of the mental process of thinking involved with the process of judging the merits of multiple options and selecting one of them for action. Some simple examples include deciding whether to get up in the morning or go back to sleep, or selecting a given route for a journey. More complex examples (often decisions that affect what a person thinks or their core beliefs) include choosing a lifestyle, religious affiliation, or political position.

   a. Championship mobilization
   b. Trade study
   c. Groups decision making
   d. Choice

4. _____ is one of the four Ps of the marketing mix. The other three aspects are product, promotion, and place. It is also a key variable in microeconomic price allocation theory.

   a. Transfer pricing
   b. Penetration pricing
   c. Price floor
   d. Pricing

5. The phrase mergers and _____s refers to the aspect of corporate strategy, corporate finance and management dealing with the buying, selling and combining of different companies that can aid, finance, or help a growing company in a given industry grow rapidly without having to create another business entity.

   An _____, also known as a takeover or a buyout, is the buying of one company (the 'target') by another. An _____ may be friendly or hostile.

   a. A4e
   b. A Stake in the Outcome
   c. AAAI
   d. Acquisition

6. _____ according to Onuoha (2007) is the practice of starting new organizations or revitalizing mature organizations, particularly new businesses generally in response to identified opportunities. _____ is often a difficult undertaking, as a vast majority of new businesses fail. Entrepreneurial activities are substantially different depending on the type of organization that is being started.

   a. A Stake in the Outcome
   b. AAAI
   c. A4e
   d. Entrepreneurship

Chapter 9. E-Commerce and the Entrepreneur

7. In economics, business, retail, and accounting, a _____ is the value of money that has been used up to produce something, and hence is not available for use anymore. In economics, a _____ is an alternative that is given up as a result of a decision. In business, the _____ may be one of acquisition, in which case the amount of money expended to acquire it is counted as _____.
    a. Cost
    b. Cost allocation
    c. Cost overrun
    d. Fixed costs

8. _____ is a term used to describe the demographic cohort following Generation X. Its members are often referred to as 'Millennials' or 'Echo Boomers') . There are no precise dates for when Gen Y begins and ends. Most commentators use dates from the early 1980s to early 1990s.
    a. Generation Y
    b. Giovanni Agnelli
    c. Benjamin R. Barber
    d. David Wittig

9. _____ is the provision of service to customers before, during and after a purchase.

According to Turban et al. (2002), '_____ is a series of activities designed to enhance the level of customer satisfaction - that is, the feeling that a product or service has met the customer expectation.'

Its importance varies by product, industry and customer; defective or broken merchandise can be exchanged, often only with a receipt and within a specified time frame.

    a. Service rate
    b. 28-hour day
    c. Customer service
    d. 1990 Clean Air Act

10. _____ is the state or fact of exclusive rights and control over property, which may be an object, land/real estate or intellectual property. An _____ right is also referred to as title. The concept of _____ has existed for thousands of years and in all cultures.
    a. A Stake in the Outcome
    b. Emanation of the state
    c. A4e
    d. Ownership

11. _____ is an advertisement in which a particular product specifically mentions a competitor by name for the express purpose of showing why the competitor is inferior to the product naming it.

This should not be confused with parody advertisements, where a fictional product is being advertised for the purpose of poking fun at the particular advertisement, nor should it be confused with the use of a coined brand name for the purpose of comparing the product without actually naming an actual competitor. ('Wikipedia tastes better and is less filling than the Encyclopedia Galactica.')

In the 1980s, during what has been referred to as the cola wars, soft-drink manufacturer Pepsi ran a series of advertisements where people, caught on hidden camera, in a blind taste test, chose Pepsi over rival Coca-Cola.

    a. 28-hour day
    b. 1990 Clean Air Act
    c. Comparative advertising
    d. 33 Strategies of War

Chapter 9. E-Commerce and the Entrepreneur

12. An _____ is a person who has possession of an enterprise and assumes significant accountability for the inherent risks and the outcome. It is an ambitious leader who combines land, labor, and capital to create and market new goods or services. The term is a loanword from French and was first defined by the Irish economist Richard Cantillon.

    a. Entrepreneur
    b. A Stake in the Outcome
    c. AAAI
    d. A4e

13. _____ , also referred to simply as a 'public offering' or 'flotation,' is when a company issues common stock or shares to the public for the first time. They are often issued by smaller, younger companies seeking capital to expand, but can also be done by large privately-owned companies looking to become publicly traded.

    In an _____ the issuer may obtain the assistance of an underwriting firm, which helps it determine what type of security to issue (common or preferred), best offering price and time to bring it to market.

    a. Unemployment insurance
    b. Initial public offering
    c. Occupational Safety and Health Administration
    d. Outsourcing

14. _____ is subcontracting a process, such as product design or manufacturing, to a third-party company. The decision to outsource is often made in the interest of lowering cost or making better use of time and energy costs, redirecting or conserving energy directed at the competencies of a particular business, or to make more efficient use of land, labor, capital, (information) technology and resources. _____ became part of the business lexicon during the 1980s.

    a. Opinion leadership
    b. Unemployment insurance
    c. Outsourcing
    d. Operant conditioning

15. _____ is something that a firm can do well and that meets the following three conditions:

    Competencies are things that companys execute well across several business units or product sectors.

    Firms usually have few competencies, but these are usually less liable to change rapidly.

    1. It provides consumer benefits
    2. It is not easy for competitors to imitate
    3. It can be leveraged widely to many products and markets.

    A _____ can take various forms, including technical/subject matter know-how, a reliable process and/or close relationships with customers and suppliers (Mascarenhas et al. 1998.)

    a. Dominant Design
    b. Learning-by-doing
    c. NAIRU
    d. Core competency

Chapter 9. E-Commerce and the Entrepreneur

16. In microeconomics, industrial organization is the field which describes the behavior of firms in the marketplace with regard to production, pricing, employment and other decisions. _____ in this field range from classical issues such as opportunity cost to neoclassical concepts such as factors of production.

- Production theory basics
    - production efficiency
    - factors of production
    - total, average, and marginal product curves
    - marginal productivity
    - isoquants ' isocosts
    - the marginal rate of technical substitution
- Economic rent
    - classical factor rents
    - Paretian factor rents
- Production possibility frontier
    - what products are possible given a set of resources
    - the trade-off between producing one product rather than another
    - the marginal rate of transformation
- Production function
    - inputs
    - diminishing returns to inputs
    - the stages of production
    - shifts in a production function
- Cost theory
    - the different types of costs
        - opportunity cost
        - accounting cost or historical costs
        - transaction cost
        - sunk cost
        - marginal cost
    - the isocost line
- Cost-of-production theory of value
- Long-run cost and production functions
    - long-run average cost
    - long-run production function and efficiency
    - returns to scale and isoclines
    - minimum efficient scale
    - plant capacity
- Economies of density
- Economies of scale
    - the efficiency consequences of increasing or decreasing the level of production
- Economies of scope
    - the efficiency consequences of increasing or decreasing the number of different types of products produced, promoted, and distributed
- Optimum factor allocation
    - output elasticity of factor costs
    - marginal revenue product
    - marginal resource cost
- Pricing
    - various aspects of the pricing decision
- Transfer pricing
    - selling within a multi-divisional company
- Joint product pricing
    - price setting when two products are linked
- Price discrimination

- o different prices to different buyers
- o types of price discrimination
- o yield management
- Price skimming
  - o price discrimination over time
- Two part tariffs
  - o charging a price composed of two parts, usually an initial fee and an ongoing fee
- Price points
  - o the effects of a non-linear demand curve on pricing
- Cost-plus pricing
  - o a markup is applied to a cost term in order to calculate price
  - o cost-plus pricing with elasticity considerations
  - o cost plus pricing is often used along with break even analysis
- Rate of return pricing
  - o calculate price based on the required rate of return on investment, or rate of return on sales
- Profit maximization
  - o determining the optimum price and quantity
  - o the totals approach
  - o marginal approach of production

a. Markup	b. Pricing
c. Price floor	d. Topics

17. _____ is an organization's process of defining its strategy and making decisions on allocating its resources to pursue this strategy, including its capital and people. Various business analysis techniques can be used in _____, including SWOT analysis (Strengths, Weaknesses, Opportunities, and Threats) and PEST analysis (Political, Economic, Social, and Technological analysis) or STEER analysis involving Socio-cultural, Technological, Economic, Ecological, and Regulatory factors and EPISTEL (Environment, Political, Informatic, Social, Technological, Economic and Legal)

_____ is the formal consideration of an organization's future course. All _____ deals with at least one of three key questions:

1. 'What do we do?'
2. 'For whom do we do it?'
3. 'How do we excel?'

In business _____, the third question is better phrased 'How can we beat or avoid competition?'. (Bradford and Duncan, page 1.)

a. 1990 Clean Air Act	b. 28-hour day
c. 33 Strategies of War	d. Strategic planning

18. A _____ is the system of organizations, people, technology, activities, information and resources involved in moving a product or service from supplier to customer. _____ activities transform natural resources, raw materials and components into a finished product that is delivered to the end customer. In sophisticated _____ systems, used products may re-enter the _____ at any point where residual value is recyclable.

a. Packaging	b. Wholesalers
c. Drop shipping	d. Supply chain

19. _____ is exchange of capital, goods, and services across international borders or territories. In most countries, it represents a significant share of gross domestic product (GDP.) While _____ has been present throughout much of history , its economic, social, and political importance has been on the rise in recent centuries.

a. A Stake in the Outcome	b. International trade
c. AAAI	d. A4e

20. An _____ is the impact an individual, business, organization or corporation has on the World Wide Web and, practicably, the traceable residue that it leaves behind through this interaction.

_____s are starting to be used to supplement interviews by some 'to research potential employees by examining what they find on the Internet.'

It also aids Law Enforcement by enabling them to get information that would be unavailable otherwise due to a lack of probable cause. More recently, with the increasing amount of data being stored on the internet it is possible to find information on someone using their Cyber Shadow/Digital Shadow.

a. A4e
c. AAAI
b. A Stake in the Outcome
d. Internet footprint

21. A _____ is a professional who provides advice in a particular area of expertise such as management, accountancy, the environment, entertainment, technology, law , human resources, marketing, medicine, finance, economics, public affairs, communication, engineering, sound system design, graphic design, or waste management.

A _____ is usually an expert or a professional in a specific field and has a wide knowledge of the subject matter. A _____ usually works for a consultancy firm or is self-employed, and engages with multiple and changing clients.

a. 33 Strategies of War
c. 28-hour day
b. 1990 Clean Air Act
d. Consultant

22. _____ is an integrated communications-based process through which individuals and communities discover that existing and newly-identified needs and wants may be satisfied by the products and services of others.

_____ is defined by the American _____ Association as the activity, set of institutions, and processes for creating, communicating, delivering, and exchanging offerings that have value for customers, clients, partners, and society at large. The term developed from the original meaning which referred literally to going to market, as in shopping, or going to a market to buy or sell goods or services.

a. Marketing
c. Market development
b. Customer relationship management
d. Disruptive technology

23. A _____ is a written document that details the necessary actions to achieve one or more marketing objectives. It can be for a product or service, a brand, or a product line. _____s cover between one and five years.

a. Market development
c. Disruptive technology
b. Marketing plan
d. Marketing strategy

24. A _____ is a process that can allow an organization to concentrate its limited resources on the greatest opportunities to increase sales and achieve a sustainable competitive advantage. A _____ should be centered around the key concept that customer satisfaction is the main goal.

A _____ is a written plan which combines product development, promotion, distribution, and pricing approach, identifies the firm's marketing goals, and explains how they will be achieved within a stated timeframe.

a. Disruptive technology
c. Marketing strategy
b. Product bundling
d. Category management

25. _____ is, in very basic words, a position a firm occupies against its competitors.

According to Michael Porter, the three methods for creating a sustainable _____ are through:

1. Cost leadership

Chapter 9. E-Commerce and the Entrepreneur 71

2. Differentiation

3. Focus (economics)

   a. 1990 Clean Air Act
   b. 28-hour day
   c. Theory Z
   d. Competitive advantage

26. _____ or promotional products refers to articles of merchandise that are used in marketing and communication programs. These items are usually imprinted with a company's name, logo or slogan, and given away at trade shows, conferences, and as part of guerrilla marketing campaigns.

Almost anything can be branded with a company's name or logo and used for promotion.

   a. 1990 Clean Air Act
   b. 28-hour day
   c. Promotional items
   d. 33 Strategies of War

27. A _____ is a formal relationship between two or more parties to pursue a set of agreed upon goals or to meet a critical business need while remaining independent organizations.

Partners may provide the _____ with resources such as products, distribution channels, manufacturing capability, project funding, capital equipment, knowledge, expertise, or intellectual property. The alliance is a cooperation or collaboration which aims for a synergy where each partner hopes that the benefits from the alliance will be greater than those from individual efforts.

   a. Process automation
   b. Strategic alliance
   c. Golden parachute
   d. Farmshoring

28. A _____ is a legal document relating to the formation of a company or corporation. It is a license to form a corporation issued by state government. Its precise meaning depends upon the legal system in which it is used, but the two primary meanings are:

- In the U.S.A. a _____ is usually used as an alternative description of a corporation's articles of incorporation.
- In English and Commonwealth legal systems, a _____ is usually a simple certificate issued by the relevant government registry as confirmation of the due incorporation and valid existence of the company.

In the U.S.A. the _____ or articles of incorporation form a major constituent part of the constitutional documents of the corporation.

   a. Civil Rights Act of 1875
   b. Toxic Substances Control Act
   c. Blue sky law
   d. Certificate of Incorporation

29. A _____ is a formal statement of a set of business goals, the reasons why they are believed attainable, and the plan for reaching those goals. It may also contain background information about the organization or team attempting to reach those goals.

The business goals may be defined for for-profit or for non-profit organizations.

a. Time management
b. Business plan
c. Distributed management
d. Crisis management

30. _____ is the activity that the selling organization undertakes to reduce customer account defections. The success of this activity is when the customer account places an additional order before a 12-month period has expired. Note that ideally these orders will need to contribute similar financial amounts to the previous 12 months.

a. Business rule
b. Foreign ownership
c. Process automation
d. Customer retention

31. In economics and sociology, an _____ is any factor (financial or non-financial) that enables or motivates a particular course of action, or counts as a reason for preferring one choice to the alternatives. It is an expectation that encourages people to behave in a certain way. Since human beings are purposeful creatures, the study of _____ structures is central to the study of all economic activity (both in terms of individual decision-making and in terms of co-operation and competition within a larger institutional structure.)

a. A4e
b. Incentive
c. AAAI
d. A Stake in the Outcome

32. _____ describes the situation when output from (or information about the result of) an event or phenomenon in the past will influence the same event/phenomenon in the present or future. When an event is part of a chain of cause-and-effect that forms a circuit or loop, then the event is said to 'feed back' into itself.

_____ is also a synonym for:

- _____ signal; the information about the initial event that is the basis for subsequent modification of the event.
- _____ loop; the causal path that leads from the initial generation of the _____ signal to the subsequent modification of the event.

_____ is a mechanism, process or signal that is looped back to control a system within itself. Such a loop is called a _____ loop.

a. Feedback loop
b. 1990 Clean Air Act
c. Positive feedback
d. Feedback

33. _____ is the measurement, collection, analysis and reporting of internet data for purposes of understanding and optimizing web usage.

There are two categories of _____; off-site and on-site _____.

Off-site _____ refers to web measurement and analysis irrespective of whether you own or maintain a website. On-site _____ measure a visitor's journey once on your website.

a. 28-hour day
b. 1990 Clean Air Act
c. Web analytics
d. 33 Strategies of War

34. _____ is the process of filtering for information or patterns using techniques involving collaboration among multiple agents, viewpoints, data sources, etc. Applications of _____ typically involve very large data sets. _____ methods have been applied to many different kinds of data including sensing and monitoring data - such as in mineral exploration, environmental sensing over large areas or multiple sensors; financial data - such as financial service institutions that integrate many financial sources; or in electronic commerce and web 2.0 applications where the focus is on user data, etc.

a. 1990 Clean Air Act
b. 28-hour day
c. 33 Strategies of War
d. Collaborative filtering

35. _____ is the intelligence of machines and the branch of computer science which aims to create it. Major _____ textbooks define the field as 'the study and design of intelligent agents,' where an intelligent agent is a system that perceives its environment and takes actions which maximize its chances of success. John McCarthy, who coined the term in 1956, defines it as 'the science and engineering of making intelligent machines.'

The field was founded on the claim that a central property of human beings, intelligence--the sapience of Homo sapiens--can be so precisely described that it can be simulated by a machine.

a. A Stake in the Outcome
b. A4e
c. AAAI
d. Artificial Intelligence

36. _____ consists of the sale of goods or merchandise from a fixed location, such as a department store, boutique or kiosk in small or individual lots for direct consumption by the purchaser. _____ may include subordinated services, such as delivery. Purchasers may be individuals or businesses.

a. 28-hour day
b. Planogram
c. 1990 Clean Air Act
d. Retailing

37. A _____ is the return of funds to a consumer, forcibly initiated by the consumer's issuing bank. Specifically, it is the reversal of a prior outbound transfer of funds from a consumer's bank account or line of credit.

The _____ mechanism exists primarily for consumer protection.

a. 33 Strategies of War
b. 1990 Clean Air Act
c. Chargeback
d. 28-hour day

Chapter 10. Pricing Strategies

1. _____ is one of the four Ps of the marketing mix. The other three aspects are product, promotion, and place. It is also a key variable in microeconomic price allocation theory.
   a. Penetration pricing
   b. Transfer pricing
   c. Price floor
   d. Pricing

2. The phrase mergers and _____s refers to the aspect of corporate strategy, corporate finance and management dealing with the buying, selling and combining of different companies that can aid, finance, or help a growing company in a given industry grow rapidly without having to create another business entity.

   An _____, also known as a takeover or a buyout, is the buying of one company (the 'target') by another. An _____ may be friendly or hostile.

   a. AAAI
   b. A4e
   c. A Stake in the Outcome
   d. Acquisition

3. _____, commonly known as e-commerce, consists of the buying and selling of products or services over electronic systems such as the Internet and other computer networks. The amount of trade conducted electronically has grown extraordinarily with widespread Internet usage. The use of commerce is conducted in this way, spurring and drawing on innovations in electronic funds transfer, supply chain management, Internet marketing, online transaction processing, electronic data interchange (EDI), inventory management systems, and automated data collection systems.
   a. Electronic Commerce
   b. A Stake in the Outcome
   c. Online shopping
   d. A4e

4. _____, or Value optimized pricing is a business strategy. It sets selling prices on the perceived value to the customer, rather than on the actual cost of the product, the market price, competitors prices, or the historical price.

   The goal of value-based pricing is to align price with value delivered.

   a. Supervisory board
   b. Chief legal officer
   c. Centralization
   d. Value based pricing

5. In economics, business, retail, and accounting, a _____ is the value of money that has been used up to produce something, and hence is not available for use anymore. In economics, a _____ is an alternative that is given up as a result of a decision. In business, the _____ may be one of acquisition, in which case the amount of money expended to acquire it is counted as _____.
   a. Cost
   b. Cost allocation
   c. Cost overrun
   d. Fixed costs

6. _____ is the state or fact of exclusive rights and control over property, which may be an object, land/real estate or intellectual property. An _____ right is also referred to as title. The concept of _____ has existed for thousands of years and in all cultures.
   a. A Stake in the Outcome
   b. Emanation of the state
   c. Ownership
   d. A4e

7. A _____ is a government imposed limit on how high a price can be charged on a product. _____s are often intended to protect consumers from certain conditions that could make necessities unattainable. But they can also cause problems if they are used for a prolonged period of time without controlled rationing.

Chapter 10. Pricing Strategies

a. Price points
b. Price ceiling
c. Price floor
d. Price discrimination

8. Why do retail stores need _____? With respect to the key objectives of growth and profit for any retail entity, _____ should significantly improve sales margins and increase sales by enabling the vendor to price variably and hence suitably and to control its product range based on profit margins. The retail stores will be able to compete more effectively with rivals in the form of mixed multiples, mail order and online retailers, who are often able to undercut but who do not generally have the same understanding of the retail market. In particular _____ is recognised as encouraging impulse buys, cross-selling of products and repeat sales.

a. 33 Strategies of War
b. 1990 Clean Air Act
c. 28-hour day
d. Dynamic pricing

9. _____ consists of the mental process of thinking involved with the process of judging the merits of multiple options and selecting one of them for action. Some simple examples include deciding whether to get up in the morning or go back to sleep, or selecting a given route for a journey. More complex examples (often decisions that affect what a person thinks or their core beliefs) include choosing a lifestyle, religious affiliation, or political position.

a. Trade study
b. Choice
c. Groups decision making
d. Championship mobilization

10. A _____ is a formal statement of a set of business goals, the reasons why they are believed attainable, and the plan for reaching those goals. It may also contain background information about the organization or team attempting to reach those goals.

The business goals may be defined for for-profit or for non-profit organizations.

a. Business plan
b. Time management
c. Distributed management
d. Crisis management

11. In economics, _____ is the desire to own something and the ability to pay for it. The term _____ signifies the ability or the willingness to buy a particular commodity at a given point of time.

a. 28-hour day
b. 33 Strategies of War
c. 1990 Clean Air Act
d. Demand

12. _____ is a lightweight markup language, originally created by John Gruber and Aaron Swartz to help maximum readability and 'publishability' of both its input and output forms. The language takes many cues from existing conventions for marking up plain text in email. _____ converts its marked-up text input to valid, well-formed XHTML and replaces left-pointing angle brackets ('<') and ampersands with their corresponding character entity references.

a. 28-hour day
b. 33 Strategies of War
c. 1990 Clean Air Act
d. Markdown

13. A _____ is a professional who provides advice in a particular area of expertise such as management, accountancy, the environment, entertainment, technology, law , human resources, marketing, medicine, finance, economics, public affairs, communication, engineering, sound system design, graphic design, or waste management.

A _____ is usually an expert or a professional in a specific field and has a wide knowledge of the subject matter. A _____ usually works for a consultancy firm or is self-employed, and engages with multiple and changing clients.

a. 28-hour day
b. 33 Strategies of War
c. Consultant
d. 1990 Clean Air Act

14. _____ is the difference between the cost of a good or service and its selling price. A _____ is added on to the total cost incurred by the producer of a good or service in order to create a profit. The total cost reflects the total amount of both fixed and variable expenses to produce and distribute a product.

a. Price points
b. Premium pricing
c. Markup
d. Topics

15. _____ is a pricing method used by companies. It is used primarily because it is easy to calculate and requires little information. There are several varieties, but the common thread in all of them is that one first calculates the cost of the product, then includes an additional amount to represent profit.

a. Cost-plus pricing
b. Price ceiling
c. Price discrimination
d. Target costing

16. _____ is one of the four elements of marketing mix. An organization or set of organizations (go-betweens) involved in the process of making a product or service available for use or consumption by a consumer or business user.

The other three parts of the marketing mix are product, pricing, and promotion.

a. Matching theory
b. Distribution
c. Missing completely at random
d. Job creation programs

17. A _____ is a process in which a potential employee is evaluated by an employer for prospective employment in their company, organization and was established in the late 16th century.

A _____ typically precedes the hiring decision, and is used to evaluate the candidate. The interview is usually preceded by the evaluation of submitted résumés from interested candidates, then selecting a small number of candidates for interviews.

a. Supported employment
b. Job interview
c. Split shift
d. Payrolling

18. _____ is an advertisement in which a particular product specifically mentions a competitor by name for the express purpose of showing why the competitor is inferior to the product naming it.

This should not be confused with parody advertisements, where a fictional product is being advertised for the purpose of poking fun at the particular advertisement, nor should it be confused with the use of a coined brand name for the purpose of comparing the product without actually naming an actual competitor. ('Wikipedia tastes better and is less filling than the Encyclopedia Galactica.')

In the 1980s, during what has been referred to as the cola wars, soft-drink manufacturer Pepsi ran a series of advertisements where people, caught on hidden camera, in a blind taste test, chose Pepsi over rival Coca-Cola.

a. 28-hour day
b. Comparative advertising
c. 33 Strategies of War
d. 1990 Clean Air Act

19. A _____ is the return of funds to a consumer, forcibly initiated by the consumer's issuing bank. Specifically, it is the reversal of a prior outbound transfer of funds from a consumer's bank account or line of credit.

The _____ mechanism exists primarily for consumer protection.

a. 1990 Clean Air Act
b. 33 Strategies of War
c. 28-hour day
d. Chargeback

20. _____ exists when one firm provides goods or services to a customer with an agreement to bill them later, or receive a shipment or service from a supplier under an agreement to pay them later. It can be viewed as an essential element of capitalization in an operating business because it can reduce the required capital investment to operate the business if it is managed properly. _____ is the largest use of capital for a majority of business to business (B2B) sellers in the United States and is a critical source of capital for a majority of all businesses.

a. Buy-sell agreement
b. Countertrade
c. 1990 Clean Air Act
d. Trade credit

Chapter 11. Creating a Successful Financial Plan

1. A _____ is a formal statement of a set of business goals, the reasons why they are believed attainable, and the plan for reaching those goals. It may also contain background information about the organization or team attempting to reach those goals.

The business goals may be defined for for-profit or for non-profit organizations.

   a. Time management
   b. Business plan
   c. Distributed management
   d. Crisis management

2. In financial accounting, a _____ or statement of financial position is a summary of a person's or organization's balances. Assets, liabilities and ownership equity are listed as of a specific date, such as the end of its financial year. A _____ is often described as a snapshot of a company's financial condition.
   a. Balance sheet
   b. 1990 Clean Air Act
   c. 33 Strategies of War
   d. 28-hour day

3. In accounting, a _____ is an asset on the balance sheet which is expected to be sold or otherwise used up in the near future, usually within one year, or one business cycle - whichever is longer. Typical _____s include cash, cash equivalents, accounts receivable, inventory, the portion of prepaid accounts which will be used within a year, and short-term investments.

On the balance sheet, assets will typically be classified into _____s and long-term assets.

   a. Matching principle
   b. Net income
   c. Treasury stock
   d. Current asset

4. _____ are formal records of the financial activities of a business, person, or other entity. In British English, including United Kingdom company law, _____ are often referred to as accounts, although the term _____ is also used, particularly by accountants.

_____ provide an overview of a business or person's financial condition in both short and long term.

   a. 1990 Clean Air Act
   b. 33 Strategies of War
   c. Financial statements
   d. 28-hour day

5. In business and accounting, _____s are everything of value that is owned by a person or company. Any property or object of value that one possesses, usually considered as applicable to the payment of one's debts is considered an _____. Simplistically stated, _____s are things of value that can be readily converted into cash.
   a. A Stake in the Outcome
   b. Asset
   c. AAAI
   d. A4e

6. The _____ is a performance management tool for measuring whether the smaller-scale operational activities of a company are aligned with its larger-scale objectives in terms of vision and strategy.

By focusing not only on financial outcomes but also on the operational, marketing and developmental inputs to these, the _____ helps provide a more comprehensive view of a business, which in turn helps organizations act in their best long-term interests. This tool is also being used to address business response to climate change and greenhouse gas emissions.

Chapter 11. Creating a Successful Financial Plan

a. Balanced scorecard
b. Middle management
c. Management development
d. Commercial management

7. _____ is a process and a set of procedures used to estimate the economic value of an owner's interest in a business. Valuation is used by financial market participants to determine the price they are willing to pay or receive to consummate a sale of a business. In addition to estimating the selling price of a business, the same valuation tools are often used by business appraisers to resolve disputes related to estate and gift taxation, divorce litigation, allocate business purchase price among business assets, establish a formula for estimating the value of partners' ownership interest for buy-sell agreements, and many other business and legal purposes.

a. No-FEAR Act
b. Munn v. Illinois
c. Business valuation
d. Robinson-Patman Act

8. In finance, _____ are considered liabilities of the business that are to be settled in cash within the fiscal year or the operating cycle, whichever period is longer.

For example accounts payable for goods, services or supplies that were purchased for use in the operation of the business and payable within a normal period of time would be _____.

Bonds, mortgages and loans that are payable over a term exceeding one year would be fixed liabilities.

a. Current liabilities
b. Matching principle
c. Generally accepted accounting principles
d. Depreciation

9. _____ , also referred to simply as a 'public offering' or 'flotation,' is when a company issues common stock or shares to the public for the first time. They are often issued by smaller, younger companies seeking capital to expand, but can also be done by large privately-owned companies looking to become publicly traded.

In an _____ the issuer may obtain the assistance of an underwriting firm, which helps it determine what type of security to issue (common or preferred), best offering price and time to bring it to market.

a. Outsourcing
b. Unemployment insurance
c. Initial public offering
d. Occupational Safety and Health Administration

10. _____ is a company's financial statement that indicates how the revenue is transformed into the net income The purpose of the _____ is to show managers and investors whether the company made or lost money during the period being reported.

The important thing to remember about an _____ is that it represents a period of time.

a. AAAI
b. Income statement
c. A Stake in the Outcome
d. A4e

11. _____ refers to the movement of cash into or out of a business or financial product. It is usually measured during a specified, finite period of time. Measurement of _____ can be used

- to determine a project's rate of return or value. The time of _____s into and out of projects are used as inputs in financial models such as internal rate of return, and net present value.
- to determine problems with a business's liquidity. Being profitable does not necessarily mean being liquid. A company can fail because of a shortage of cash, even while profitable.
- as an alternate measure of a business's profits when it is believed that accrual accounting concepts do not represent economic realities. For example, a company may be notionally profitable but generating little operational cash (as may be the case for a company that barters its products rather than selling for cash.) In such a case, the company may be deriving additional operating cash by issuing shares evaluating default risk, re-investment requirements, etc.

_____ is a generic term used differently depending on the context. It may be defined by users for their own purposes.

a. Gross profit margin
b. Gross profit
c. Sweat equity
d. Cash flow

12. In accounting, _____ or sales profit is the difference between revenue and the cost of making a product or providing a service, before deducting overhead, payroll, taxation, and interest payments. Note that this is different from operating profit (earnings before interest and taxes.)

Net sales are calculated:

Net sales = Sales - Sales returns and allowances.

a. Capital budgeting
b. Gross profit margin
c. Cash flow
d. Gross profit

13. _____ is a financial ratio used to assess the profitability of a firm's core activities, excluding fixed costs.

The general calculation is:

The _____ is related to the net profit margin, which assesses the profitability of an organization after including fixed costs.

_____ indicates the relationship between net sales revenue and the cost of goods sold.

a. Capital structure
b. Shareholder value
c. Sweat equity
d. Gross profit margin

Chapter 11. Creating a Successful Financial Plan

14. An _____, operating expenditure, operational expense, operational expenditure or OPEX is an on-going cost for running a product, business, or system. Its counterpart, a capital expenditure (CAPEX), is the cost of developing or providing non-consumable parts for the product or system. For example, the purchase of a photocopier is the CAPEX, and the annual paper and toner cost is the OPEX.
    a. Operating expense
    b. A Stake in the Outcome
    c. AAAI
    d. A4e

15. _____, net margin, net _____ or net profit ratio all refer to a measure of profitability. It is calculated by finding the net profit as a percentage of the revenue.

$$\text{Net profit margin} = \frac{\text{Net profit (after taxes)}}{\text{Revenue}} \times 100\%$$

The _____ is mostly used for internal comparison.

   a. 1990 Clean Air Act
   b. Profit maximization
   c. Net profit margin
   d. Profit margin

16. A _____ is a professional who provides advice in a particular area of expertise such as management, accountancy, the environment, entertainment, technology, law, human resources, marketing, medicine, finance, economics, public affairs, communication, engineering, sound system design, graphic design, or waste management.

A _____ is usually an expert or a professional in a specific field and has a wide knowledge of the subject matter. A _____ usually works for a consultancy firm or is self-employed, and engages with multiple and changing clients.

   a. 28-hour day
   b. 1990 Clean Air Act
   c. 33 Strategies of War
   d. Consultant

17. _____ is the state or fact of exclusive rights and control over property, which may be an object, land/real estate or intellectual property. An _____ right is also referred to as title. The concept of _____ has existed for thousands of years and in all cultures.
   a. A4e
   b. A Stake in the Outcome
   c. Emanation of the state
   d. Ownership

18. _____ is one of the four Ps of the marketing mix. The other three aspects are product, promotion, and place. It is also a key variable in microeconomic price allocation theory.
   a. Price floor
   b. Pricing
   c. Transfer pricing
   d. Penetration pricing

19. In economics, business, retail, and accounting, a _____ is the value of money that has been used up to produce something, and hence is not available for use anymore. In economics, a _____ is an alternative that is given up as a result of a decision. In business, the _____ may be one of acquisition, in which case the amount of money expended to acquire it is counted as _____.

Chapter 11. Creating a Successful Financial Plan

a. Cost allocation
b. Fixed costs
c. Cost overrun
d. Cost

20. The _____ is a financial ratio that measures whether or not a firm has enough resources to pay its debts over the next 12 months. It compares a firm's current assets to its current liabilities. It is expressed as follows:

$$\text{Current ratio} = \frac{\text{Current Assets}}{\text{Current Liabilities}}$$

For example, if WXY Company's current assets are $50,000,000 and its current liabilities are $40,000,000, then its _____ would be $50,000,000 divided by $40,000,000, which equals 1.25.

a. Return on assets
b. Financial ratio
c. Times interest earned
d. Current ratio

21. Market _____ is a business, economics or investment term that refers to an asset's ability to be easily converted through an act of buying or selling without causing a significant movement in the price and with minimum loss of value. Money, or cash on hand, is the most liquid asset. An act of exchange of a less liquid asset with a more liquid asset is called liquidation.

a. 28-hour day
b. Liquidity
c. 1990 Clean Air Act
d. 33 Strategies of War

22. In finance, the _____ or quick ratio or liquid ratio measures the ability of a company to use its near cash or quick assets to immediately extinguish or retire its current liabilities. Quick assets include those current assets that presumably can be quickly converted to cash at close to their book values.

Generally, the acid test ratio should be 1:1 or better, however this varies widely by industry.

a. Inventory turnover
b. A4e
c. A Stake in the Outcome
d. Acid-test

23. In finance, _____ is borrowing money to supplement existing funds for investment in such a way that the potential positive or negative outcome is magnified and/or enhanced. It generally refers to using borrowed funds, or debt, so as to attempt to increase the returns to equity. Deleveraging is the action of reducing borrowings.

a. Private equity
b. Limited partners
c. Limited liability corporation
d. Gearing

24. _____ is a financial ratio that indicates the percentage of a company's assets are provided via debt. It is the ratio of total debt (the sum of current liabilities and long-term liabilities) and total assets (the sum of current assets, fixed assets, and other assets such as 'goodwill'.)

$$\text{Debt ratio} = \frac{\text{Total Debt}}{\text{Total Assets}}$$

or alternatively:

$$\text{Debt ratio} = \frac{\text{Total Liability}}{\text{Total Assets}}$$

For example, a company with $2 million in total assets and $500,000 in total liabilities would have a _____ of 25%

Like all financial ratios, a company's _____ should be compared with their industry average or other competing firms.

a. Demand forecasting
b. 28-hour day
c. Debt ratio
d. 1990 Clean Air Act

25. In business, _____ is the total liabilities minus total outside assets of an individual or a company. For a company, this is called shareholders' preference and may be referred to as book value. _____ is stated as at a particular year in time.
a. Payback period
b. Novated lease
c. Deferred compensation
d. Net worth

26. _____ or interest coverage ratio is a measure of a company's ability to honor its debt payments. It may be calculated as either EBIT or EBITDA divided by the total interest payable.

a. Return on sales
b. P/E ratio
c. Rate of return
d. Times interest earned

27. The _____ is a financial term defined as a company's operating expenses as a percentage of revenue. This financial ratio is most commonly used for industries such as railroads which require a large percentage of revenues to maintain operations. In railroading, an _____ of 80 or lower is considered desirable.
a. A Stake in the Outcome
b. A4e
c. AAAI
d. Operating ratio

28. The _____ is an equation that equals the cost of goods sold divided by the average inventory. Average inventory equals beginning inventory plus ending inventory divided by 2.

The formula for _____:

The formula for average inventory:

A low turnover rate may point to overstocking, obsolescence, or deficiencies in the product line or marketing effort.

a. A4e
b. A Stake in the Outcome
c. Inventory turnover
d. Asset turnover

29. _____ is one of the Accounting Liquidity ratios, a financial ratio. This ratio measures the number of times, on average, the inventory is sold during the period. Its purpose is to measure the liquidity of the inventory.

a. A4e
b. A Stake in the Outcome
c. Inventory
d. Inventory turnover ratio

30. In a human resources context, _____ or labor _____ is the rate at which an employer gains and loses employees. Simple ways to describe it are 'how long employees tend to stay' or 'the rate of traffic through the revolving door.' _____ is measured for individual companies and for their industry as a whole. If an employer is said to have a high _____ relative to its competitors, it means that employees of that company have a shorter average tenure than those of other companies in the same industry.

a. Ten year occupational employment projection
b. Career portfolios
c. Continuous
d. Turnover

31. In business and finance accounting, _____ is equal to the gross profit minus overheads minus interest payable plus/minus one off items for a given time period (usually: accounting period.)

A common synonym for '_____' when discussing financial statements (which include a balance sheet and an income statement) is the bottom line. This term results from the traditional appearance of an income statement which shows all allocated revenues and expenses over a specified time period with the resulting summation on the bottom line of the report.

a. Matching principle
b. Generally accepted accounting principles
c. Treasury stock
d. Net profit

32. The _____ is a measure of how revenue growth translates into growth in operating income. It is a measure of leverage, and of how risky (volatile) a company's operating income is.

There are various measures of _____, which can be interpreted analogously to financial leverage.

a. A Stake in the Outcome
b. AAAI
c. A4e
d. Operating leverage

Chapter 11. Creating a Successful Financial Plan

33. In decision theory and estimation theory, the _____ of an estimator, $\hat{\theta}$, of an unknown parameter of the distribution, θ, is the expected value of the loss function

$$R(\theta, \hat{\theta}) = \mathbb{E}_\theta L(\theta, \hat{\theta}) = \int L(\theta, \hat{\theta}) \, dP_\theta.$$

where dP_θ is a probability measure parametrized by θ.

- For a scalar parameter θ and a quadratic loss function,

$$L(\theta, \hat{\theta}) = (\theta - \hat{\theta})^2$$

the _____ function becomes the mean squared error of the estimate,

$$R(\theta, \hat{\theta}) = E_\theta (\theta - \hat{\theta})^2$$

- In density estimation, the unknown parameter is probability density itself. The loss function is typically chosen to be a norm in an appropriate function space. For example, for L^2 norm,

$$L(f, \hat{f}) = \|f - \hat{f}\|_2^2$$

the _____ function becomes the mean integrated squared error

$$R(f, \hat{f}) = E\|f - \hat{f}\|^2$$

a. Risk aversion
b. Financial modeling
c. Linear model
d. Risk

34. In finance, a _____ or accounting ratio is a ratio of two selected numerical values taken from an enterprise's financial statements. There are many standard ratios used to try to evaluate the overall financial condition of a corporation or other organization. _____s may be used by managers within a firm, by current and potential shareholders (owners) of a firm, and by a firm's creditors.
   a. Financial Ratio
   b. Return on equity
   c. Return on sales
   d. Rate of return

35. _____ is a mathematical science pertaining to the collection, analysis, interpretation or explanation, and presentation of data. It also provides tools for prediction and forecasting based on data. It is applicable to a wide variety of academic disciplines, from the natural and social sciences to the humanities, government and business.
   a. Simple moving average
   b. Location parameter
   c. Failure rate
   d. Statistics

36. An _____ is an organization founded and funded by businesses that operate in a specific industry. An industry trade association participates in public relations activities such as advertising, education, political donations, lobbying and publishing, but its main focus is collaboration between companies, or standardization. Associations may offer other services, such as producing conferences, networking or charitable events or offering classes or educational materials.

   a. AAAI
   b. A4e
   c. A Stake in the Outcome
   d. Industry trade group

37. In economics ' business, specifically cost accounting, the _____ is the point at which cost or expenses and revenue are equal: there is no net loss or gain, and one has 'broken even'. A profit or a loss has not been made, although opportunity costs have been paid, and capital has received the risk-adjusted, expected return.

For example, if the business sells less than 200 tables each month, it will make a loss, if it sells more, it will be a profit.

   a. Defined benefit pension plan
   b. Break-even point
   c. Fixed asset turnover
   d. Virtuous circle

38. _____ is a file or account that contains money that a person or company owes to suppliers, but has not paid yet (a form of debt.) When you receive an invoice you add it to the file, and then you remove it when you pay. Thus, the A/P is a form of credit that suppliers offer to their purchasers by allowing them to pay for a product or service after it has already been received.

   a. Accounts payable
   b. A Stake in the Outcome
   c. Other revenue
   d. Accounts receivable

Chapter 12. Managing Cash Flow

1. A _____ is a formal statement of a set of business goals, the reasons why they are believed attainable, and the plan for reaching those goals. It may also contain background information about the organization or team attempting to reach those goals.

The business goals may be defined for for-profit or for non-profit organizations.

   a. Business Plan
   b. Distributed management
   c. Time management
   d. Crisis management

2. _____ is the process of estimation in unknown situations. Prediction is a similar, but more general term. Both can refer to estimation of time series, cross-sectional or longitudinal data.
   a. 33 Strategies of War
   b. 1990 Clean Air Act
   c. 28-hour day
   d. Forecasting

3. _____ refers to the movement of cash into or out of a business or financial product. It is usually measured during a specified, finite period of time. Measurement of _____ can be used

   - to determine a project's rate of return or value. The time of _____s into and out of projects are used as inputs in financial models such as internal rate of return, and net present value.
   - to determine problems with a business's liquidity. Being profitable does not necessarily mean being liquid. A company can fail because of a shortage of cash, even while profitable.
   - as an alternate measure of a business's profits when it is believed that accrual accounting concepts do not represent economic realities. For example, a company may be notionally profitable but generating little operational cash (as may be the case for a company that barters its products rather than selling for cash.) In such a case, the company may be deriving additional operating cash by issuing shares evaluating default risk, re-investment requirements, etc.

_____ is a generic term used differently depending on the context. It may be defined by users for their own purposes.

   a. Gross profit margin
   b. Gross profit
   c. Sweat equity
   d. Cash flow

4. _____ generally refers to a list of all planned expenses and revenues. It is a plan for saving and spending. A _____ is an important concept in microeconomics, which uses a _____ line to illustrate the trade-offs between two or more goods.
   a. 33 Strategies of War
   b. Budget
   c. 1990 Clean Air Act
   d. 28-hour day

5. A _____ is a professional who provides advice in a particular area of expertise such as management, accountancy, the environment, entertainment, technology, law , human resources, marketing, medicine, finance, economics, public affairs, communication, engineering, sound system design, graphic design, or waste management.

A _____ is usually an expert or a professional in a specific field and has a wide knowledge of the subject matter. A _____ usually works for a consultancy firm or is self-employed, and engages with multiple and changing clients.

Chapter 12. Managing Cash Flow

a. Consultant
b. 28-hour day
c. 33 Strategies of War
d. 1990 Clean Air Act

6. The _____ is a performance management tool for measuring whether the smaller-scale operational activities of a company are aligned with its larger-scale objectives in terms of vision and strategy.

By focusing not only on financial outcomes but also on the operational, marketing and developmental inputs to these, the _____ helps provide a more comprehensive view of a business, which in turn helps organizations act in their best long-term interests. This tool is also being used to address business response to climate change and greenhouse gas emissions.

a. Management development
b. Middle management
c. Balanced scorecard
d. Commercial management

7. _____ is the state or fact of exclusive rights and control over property, which may be an object, land/real estate or intellectual property. An _____ right is also referred to as title. The concept of _____ has existed for thousands of years and in all cultures.
a. A4e
b. A Stake in the Outcome
c. Emanation of the state
d. Ownership

8. _____ is one of a series of accounting transactions dealing with the billing of customers who owe money to a person, company or organization for goods and services that have been provided to the customer. In most business entities this is typically done by generating an invoice and mailing or electronically delivering it to the customer, who in turn must pay it within an established timeframe called credit or payment terms.

An example of a common payment term is Net 30, meaning payment is due in the amount of the invoice 30 days from the date of invoice.

a. Accumulated Depreciation
b. Accounts receivable
c. A Stake in the Outcome
d. Other revenue

9. _____ is a file or account that contains money that a person or company owes to suppliers, but has not paid yet (a form of debt.) When you receive an invoice you add it to the file, and then you remove it when you pay. Thus, the A/P is a form of credit that suppliers offer to their purchasers by allowing them to pay for a product or service after it has already been received.
a. Accounts receivable
b. Other revenue
c. A Stake in the Outcome
d. Accounts payable

10. A _____ is typically described as a deliberate plan of action to guide decisions and achieve rational outcome(s.) However, the term may also be used to denote what is actually done, even though it is unplanned.

The term may apply to government, private sector organizations and groups, and individuals.

a. Policy
b. 1990 Clean Air Act
c. 33 Strategies of War
d. 28-hour day

Chapter 12. Managing Cash Flow

11. In physics, and more specifically kinematics, _____ is the change in velocity over time. Because velocity is a vector, it can change in two ways: a change in magnitude and/or a change in direction. In one dimension, _____ is the rate at which something speeds up or slows down.
    a. Acceleration
    b. AAAI
    c. A Stake in the Outcome
    d. A4e

12. The _____, first published in 1952, is one of a number of uniform acts that have been promulgated in conjunction with efforts to harmonize the law of sales and other commercial transactions in all 50 states within the United States of America. This objective is deemed important because of the prevalence of commercial transactions that extend beyond one state (for example, where the goods are manufactured in state A, warehoused in state B, sold from state C and delivered in state D.) The _____ deals primarily with transactions involving personal property (movable property), not real property (immovable property.)
    a. A Stake in the Outcome
    b. A4e
    c. Uniform Commercial Code
    d. AAAI

13. _____ is a marketing method by which business opportunities are created through networks of like-minded business people. There are several prominent _____ organizations that create models of networking activity that, when followed, allow the business person to build new business relationship and generate business opportunities at the same time.

    Many business people contend _____ is a more cost-effective method of generating new business than advertising or public relations efforts.

    a. Business networking
    b. Cross-selling
    c. Business model design
    d. Yield management

14. A _____ is a business that is privately owned and operated, with a small number of employees and relatively low volume of sales. The legal definition of 'small' often varies by country and industry, but is generally under 100 employees in the United States and under 50 employees in the European Union. In comparison, the definition of mid-sized business by the number of employees is generally under 500 in the U.S. and 250 for the European Union.
    a. Golden Boot Compensation
    b. Pre-determined overhead rate
    c. Critical Success Factor
    d. Small Business

15. In a human resources context, _____ or labor _____ is the rate at which an employer gains and loses employees. Simple ways to describe it are 'how long employees tend to stay' or 'the rate of traffic through the revolving door.' _____ is measured for individual companies and for their industry as a whole. If an employer is said to have a high _____ relative to its competitors, it means that employees of that company have a shorter average tenure than those of other companies in the same industry.
    a. Career portfolios
    b. Ten year occupational employment projection
    c. Continuous
    d. Turnover

16. _____ or promotional products refers to articles of merchandise that are used in marketing and communication programs. These items are usually imprinted with a company's name, logo or slogan, and given away at trade shows, conferences, and as part of guerrilla marketing campaigns.

    Almost anything can be branded with a company's name or logo and used for promotion.

Chapter 12. Managing Cash Flow

a. 28-hour day
b. 1990 Clean Air Act
c. 33 Strategies of War
d. Promotional items

17. _____ , also referred to simply as a 'public offering' or 'flotation,' is when a company issues common stock or shares to the public for the first time. They are often issued by smaller, younger companies seeking capital to expand, but can also be done by large privately-owned companies looking to become publicly traded.

In an _____ the issuer may obtain the assistance of an underwriting firm, which helps it determine what type of security to issue (common or preferred), best offering price and time to bring it to market.

a. Outsourcing
b. Unemployment insurance
c. Occupational Safety and Health Administration
d. Initial public offering

18. In business, overhead, _____ or overhead expense refers to an ongoing expense of operating a business. The term overhead is usually used to group expenses that are necessary to the continued functioning of the business, but do not directly generate profits.

Overhead expenses are all costs on the income statement except for direct labor and direct materials.

a. Overhead cost
b. Industrial market segmentation
c. Intangible assets
d. Interlocking directorate

19. In economics, business, retail, and accounting, a _____ is the value of money that has been used up to produce something, and hence is not available for use anymore. In economics, a _____ is an alternative that is given up as a result of a decision. In business, the _____ may be one of acquisition, in which case the amount of money expended to acquire it is counted as _____.

a. Cost overrun
b. Cost
c. Cost allocation
d. Fixed costs

20. _____ is one of the four Ps of the marketing mix. The other three aspects are product, promotion, and place. It is also a key variable in microeconomic price allocation theory.

a. Transfer pricing
b. Penetration pricing
c. Price floor
d. Pricing

21. A _____ is a provisional group of workers who work for an organization on a non-permanent basis independent professionals, temporary contract workers, independent contractors or consultants. _____ Management is the strategic approach to managing an organization's _____ in a way that it reduces the company's cost in the management of contingent employees and mitigates the company's risk in employing them.

According to the US Bureau of Labor Statistics, the nontraditional workforce includes 'multiple job holders, contingent and part-time workers, and people in alternative work arrangements.' These workers currently represent a substantial portion of the U.S. workforce, and 'nearly four out of five employers, in establishments of all sizes and industries, use some form of nontraditional staffing.' 'People in alternative work arrangements' includes independent contractors, employees of contract companies, workers who are on call, and temporary workers.

a. 1990 Clean Air Act
b. 33 Strategies of War
c. Contingent workforce
d. 28-hour day

22. _____ is subcontracting a process, such as product design or manufacturing, to a third-party company. The decision to outsource is often made in the interest of lowering cost or making better use of time and energy costs, redirecting or conserving energy directed at the competencies of a particular business, or to make more efficient use of land, labor, capital, (information) technology and resources. _____ became part of the business lexicon during the 1980s.
 a. Operant conditioning
 b. Opinion leadership
 c. Unemployment insurance
 d. Outsourcing

23. The _____ is the labour pool in employment. It is generally used to describe those working for a single company or industry, but can also apply to a geographic region like a city, country, state, etc. The term generally excludes the employers or management, and implies those involved in manual labour.
 a. Division of labour
 b. Work-life balance
 c. Pink-collar worker
 d. Workforce

24. _____ is a technique of planning and decision-making which reverses the working process of traditional budgeting. In traditional incremental budgeting, departmental managers justify only increases over the previous year budget and what has been already spent is automatically sanctioned. No reference is made to the previous level of expenditure.
 a. 33 Strategies of War
 b. 28-hour day
 c. Zero-based budgeting
 d. 1990 Clean Air Act

25. _____, commonly known as e-commerce, consists of the buying and selling of products or services over electronic systems such as the Internet and other computer networks. The amount of trade conducted electronically has grown extraordinarily with widespread Internet usage. The use of commerce is conducted in this way, spurring and drawing on innovations in electronic funds transfer, supply chain management, Internet marketing, online transaction processing, electronic data interchange (EDI), inventory management systems, and automated data collection systems.
 a. A4e
 b. A Stake in the Outcome
 c. Online shopping
 d. Electronic Commerce

Chapter 13. Sources of Financing: Debt and Equity

1. A _____ is a formal statement of a set of business goals, the reasons why they are believed attainable, and the plan for reaching those goals. It may also contain background information about the organization or team attempting to reach those goals.

The business goals may be defined for for-profit or for non-profit organizations.

a. Time management
c. Distributed management
b. Business Plan
d. Crisis management

2. An _____ is an overview of an idea for a product, service, or project. The name reflects the fact that an _____ can be delivered in the time span of an elevator ride (for example, thirty seconds and 100-150 words).

The term is typically used in the context of an entrepreneur pitching an idea to a venture capitalist or angel investor to receive funding.

a. Elevator pitch
c. A4e
b. AAAI
d. A Stake in the Outcome

3. _____ consists of the mental process of thinking involved with the process of judging the merits of multiple options and selecting one of them for action. Some simple examples include deciding whether to get up in the morning or go back to sleep, or selecting a given route for a journey. More complex examples (often decisions that affect what a person thinks or their core beliefs) include choosing a lifestyle, religious affiliation, or political position.

a. Groups decision making
c. Trade study
b. Championship mobilization
d. Choice

4. _____ is a type of private equity investment, most often a minority investment, in relatively mature companies that are looking for capital to expand or restructure operations, enter new markets or finance a significant acquisition without a change of control of the business.

Companies that seek _____, will often do so in order to finance a transformational event in their lifecycle. These companies are likely to be more mature than venture capital funded companies, able to generate revenue and operating profits but unable to generate sufficient cash to fund major expansions, acquisitions or other investments.

a. Pension fund
c. Growth capital
b. Seed round
d. Management buyout

5. _____ , also referred to simply as a 'public offering' or 'flotation,' is when a company issues common stock or shares to the public for the first time. They are often issued by smaller, younger companies seeking capital to expand, but can also be done by large privately-owned companies looking to become publicly traded.

In an _____ the issuer may obtain the assistance of an underwriting firm, which helps it determine what type of security to issue (common or preferred), best offering price and time to bring it to market.

a. Unemployment insurance
c. Outsourcing
b. Occupational Safety and Health Administration
d. Initial public offering

Chapter 13. Sources of Financing: Debt and Equity

6. _____ is a financial metric which represents operating liquidity available to a business. Along with fixed assets such as plant and equipment, _____ is considered a part of operating capital. It is calculated as current assets minus current liabilities.
   a. Working capital
   b. 1990 Clean Air Act
   c. 33 Strategies of War
   d. 28-hour day

7. _____ is the capital that a business raises by taking out a loan. It is a loan made to a company that is normally repaid at some future date. _____ differs from equity or share capital because subscribers to _____ do not become part owners of the business, but are merely creditors, and the suppliers of _____ usually receive a contractually fixed annual percentage return on their loan, and this is known as the coupon rate.
   a. Novated lease
   b. Net worth
   c. Market value added
   d. Debt capital

8. _____ is a civil designation for persons who are incorporated in a fixed or permanent way to a society or group: regular member of the working staff, permanent staff distinguished from a supernumerary.

The term '_____' and its counterpart, 'supernumerary,' originated in Spanish and Latin American academy and government; it is now also used in countries all over the world, such as France, the U.S., England, Italy, etc.

There are _____ members of surgical organizations, of universities, of gastronomical associations, etc.

   a. Adam Smith
   b. Abraham Harold Maslow
   c. Affiliation
   d. Numerary

9. _____ is the state or fact of exclusive rights and control over property, which may be an object, land/real estate or intellectual property. An _____ right is also referred to as title. The concept of _____ has existed for thousands of years and in all cultures.
   a. Emanation of the state
   b. A4e
   c. A Stake in the Outcome
   d. Ownership

10. An _____ is any party that makes an investment.

The term has taken on a specific meaning in finance to describe the particular types of people and companies that regularly purchase equity or debt securities for financial gain in exchange for funding an expanding company. Less frequently, the term is applied to parties who purchase real estate, currency, commodity derivatives, personal property, or other assets.

   a. A Stake in the Outcome
   b. Investor
   c. AAAI
   d. A4e

11. A _____, sometimes known as a friends and family round or seed funding, is a securities offering whereby one or more parties that have some connection to a new enterprise invest the funds necessary to start the business so that it has enough funds to sustain itself for a period of development until it reaches either a state where it is able to continue funding itself, or has created something in value so that it is worthy of future rounds of funding. Seed money refers to the money so invested.

Chapter 13. Sources of Financing: Debt and Equity

a. Seed round
b. Limited partnership
c. Limited liability corporation
d. Venture Capitalist

12. A _____ is a type of business entity in which partners (owners) share with each other the profits or losses of the business. _____s are often favored over corporations for taxation purposes, as the _____ structure does not generally incur a tax on profits before it is distributed to the partners (i.e. there is no dividend tax levied.) However, depending on the _____ structure and the jurisdiction in which it operates, owners of a _____ may be exposed to greater personal liability than they would as shareholders of a corporation.

a. Mediation
b. Due process
c. Federal Employers Liability Act
d. Partnership

13. An _____ is a person who has possession of an enterprise and assumes significant accountability for the inherent risks and the outcome. It is an ambitious leader who combines land, labor, and capital to create and market new goods or services. The term is a loanword from French and was first defined by the Irish economist Richard Cantillon.

a. Entrepreneur
b. AAAI
c. A Stake in the Outcome
d. A4e

14. _____ is a type of private equity capital typically provided to early-stage, high-potential, growth companies in the interest of generating a return through an eventual realization event such as an IPO or trade sale of the company. _____ investments are generally made as cash in exchange for shares in the invested company. It is typical for _____ investors to identify and back companies in high technology industries such as biotechnology and ICT.

a. Seed round
b. Venture capital
c. Private equity
d. Limited liability corporation

15. An _____, for United States federal income tax purposes, is a corporation that makes a valid election to be taxed under Subchapter S of Chapter 1 of the Internal Revenue Code.

In general, _____s do not pay any income taxes. Instead, the corporation's income or losses are divided among and passed through to its shareholders.

a. S corporation
b. 1990 Clean Air Act
c. 33 Strategies of War
d. 28-hour day

16. The _____ is a bank regulation, which sets a framework on how banks and depository institutions must handle their capital. The categorization of assets and capital is highly standardized so that it can be risk weighted. Internationally, the Basel Committee on Banking Supervision housed at the Bank for International Settlements influence each country's banking _____s.

a. Lock box
b. 1990 Clean Air Act
c. Reserve requirement
d. Capital requirement

17. The U.S. _____ is an independent agency of the United States government which holds primary responsibility for enforcing the federal securities laws and regulating the securities industry, the nation's stock and options exchanges, and other electronic securities markets. The SEC was created by section 4 of the Securities Exchange Act of 1934 (now codified as 15 U.S.C. Â§ 78d and commonly referred to as the 1934 Act.)

Chapter 13. Sources of Financing: Debt and Equity

a. 1990 Clean Air Act
b. 28-hour day
c. 33 Strategies of War
d. Securities and Exchange Commission

18. A _____ refers to how a corporation is perceived. It is a generally accepted image of what a company 'stands for'. The creation of a _____ is an exercise in perception management.
   a. Marketing
   b. Corporate image
   c. Market development
   d. Context analysis

19. _____ is a concept in ethics with several meanings. It is often used synonymously with such concepts as responsibility, answerability, enforcement, blameworthiness, liability and other terms associated with the expectation of account-giving. As an aspect of governance, it has been central to discussions related to problems in both the public and private (corporation) worlds.
   a. A Stake in the Outcome
   b. Usury
   c. Accountability
   d. A4e

20. The _____ of 2002 (Pub.L. 107-204, 116 Stat. 745, enacted July 30, 2002), also known as the Public Company Accounting Reform and Investor Protection Act of 2002 and commonly called Sarbanes-Oxley, Sarbox or SOX, is a United States federal law enacted on July 30, 2002, as a reaction to a number of major corporate and accounting scandals including those affecting Enron, Tyco International, Adelphia, Peregrine Systems and WorldCom.
   a. Fair Labor Standards Act
   b. Letter of credit
   c. Sarbanes-Oxley Act of 2002
   d. Sarbanes-Oxley Act

21. A mutual _____ or stockholder is an individual or company (including a corporation) that legally owns one or more shares of stock in a joint stock company. A company's _____s collectively own that company. Thus, the typical goal of such companies is to enhance _____ value.
   a. Stockholder
   b. Shareholder
   c. 1990 Clean Air Act
   d. Free riding

22. Under the Securities Act of 1933, any offer to sell securities must either be registered with the SEC or meet an exemption. _____ contains three rules providing exemptions from the registration requirements, allowing some companies to offer and sell their securities without having to register the securities with the SEC. Rule 501 of Reg D contains definitions that apply to the rest of Reg D. Rule 502 contains the general conditions that must be met to take advantage of the exemptions under _____. Generally speaking, these conditions are (1) that all sales within a certain time period that are part of the same Reg D offering must be 'integrated', meaning they must be treated as one offering, (2) information and disclosures must be provided, (3) there must be no 'general solicitation', and (4) that the securities being sold contain restrictions on their resale.
   a. 28-hour day
   b. 33 Strategies of War
   c. Regulation D
   d. 1990 Clean Air Act

23. _____-model (SCOR(r)) is a process reference model developed by the management consulting firm PRTM and AMR Research and endorsed by the Supply-Chain Council (SCC) as the cross-industry de facto standard diagnostic tool for supply chain management. SCOR enables users to address, improve, and communicate supply chain management practices within and between all interested parties in the Extended Enterprise.

Chapter 13. Sources of Financing: Debt and Equity

SCOR(r) is a management tool, spanning from the supplier's supplier to the customer's customer. The model has been developed by the members of the Council on a volunteer basis to describe the business activities associated with all phases of satisfying a customer's demand.

a. Supply chain management software
b. Supply Chain Risk Management
c. Delayed differentiation
d. Supply-Chain Operations Reference

24. A _____ is a professional who provides advice in a particular area of expertise such as management, accountancy, the environment, entertainment, technology, law, human resources, marketing, medicine, finance, economics, public affairs, communication, engineering, sound system design, graphic design, or waste management.

A _____ is usually an expert or a professional in a specific field and has a wide knowledge of the subject matter. A _____ usually works for a consultancy firm or is self-employed, and engages with multiple and changing clients.

a. Consultant
b. 28-hour day
c. 33 Strategies of War
d. 1990 Clean Air Act

25. A _____ is a business that is privately owned and operated, with a small number of employees and relatively low volume of sales. The legal definition of 'small' often varies by country and industry, but is generally under 100 employees in the United States and under 50 employees in the European Union. In comparison, the definition of mid-sized business by the number of employees is generally under 500 in the U.S. and 250 for the European Union.

a. Small business
b. Critical Success Factor
c. Pre-determined overhead rate
d. Golden Boot Compensation

26. A _____ is any credit source extended to a business by a bank or financial institution. A _____ may take several forms such as cash credit, overdraft, demand loan, export packing credit, term loan, discounting or purchase of commercial bills etc. It is like an account that can readily be tapped into if the need arises or not touched at all and saved for emergencies.

a. Line of credit
b. 33 Strategies of War
c. 1990 Clean Air Act
d. 28-hour day

27. Title _____s serve as guarantees to the recipient of property, ensuring that the recipient receives what he or she bargained for. The English _____s of title, sometimes included in deeds to real property, are that the grantor is lawfully seized (in fee simple) of the property, (2) that the grantor has the right to convey the property to the grantee, (3) that the property is conveyed without encumbrances (this _____ is frequently modified to allow for certain encumbrances), (4) that the grantor has done no act to encumber the property, (5) that the grantee shall have quiet possession of the property, and (6) that the grantor will execute such further assurances of the land as may be requisite (Nos. 3 and 4, which overlap significantly, are sometimes treated as one item.)

a. Trade secret
b. Business valuation
c. Hostile work environment
d. Covenant

Chapter 13. Sources of Financing: Debt and Equity

28. _____ according to Onuoha (2007) is the practice of starting new organizations or revitalizing mature organizations, particularly new businesses generally in response to identified opportunities. _____ is often a difficult undertaking, as a vast majority of new businesses fail. Entrepreneurial activities are substantially different depending on the type of organization that is being started.
   a. AAAI
   b. A4e
   c. A Stake in the Outcome
   d. Entrepreneurship

29. _____ is one of a series of accounting transactions dealing with the billing of customers who owe money to a person, company or organization for goods and services that have been provided to the customer. In most business entities this is typically done by generating an invoice and mailing or electronically delivering it to the customer, who in turn must pay it within an established timeframe called credit or payment terms.

An example of a common payment term is Net 30, meaning payment is due in the amount of the invoice 30 days from the date of invoice.

   a. A Stake in the Outcome
   b. Other revenue
   c. Accumulated Depreciation
   d. Accounts receivable

30. _____ is a form of short-term borrowing often used to improve a company's working capital and cash flow position.

_____ allows a business to draw money against its sales invoices before the customer has actually paid. To do this, the business borrows a percentage of the value of its sales ledger from a finance company, effectively using the unpaid sales invoices as collateral for the borrowing.

   a. AAAI
   b. A4e
   c. A Stake in the Outcome
   d. Invoice discounting

31. In a human resources context, _____ or labor _____ is the rate at which an employer gains and loses employees. Simple ways to describe it are 'how long employees tend to stay' or 'the rate of traffic through the revolving door.' _____ is measured for individual companies and for their industry as a whole. If an employer is said to have a high _____ relative to its competitors, it means that employees of that company have a shorter average tenure than those of other companies in the same industry.
   a. Ten year occupational employment projection
   b. Turnover
   c. Career portfolios
   d. Continuous

32. _____ exists when one firm provides goods or services to a customer with an agreement to bill them later, or receive a shipment or service from a supplier under an agreement to pay them later. It can be viewed as an essential element of capitalization in an operating business because it can reduce the required capital investment to operate the business if it is managed properly. _____ is the largest use of capital for a majority of business to business (B2B) sellers in the United States and is a critical source of capital for a majority of all businesses.
   a. Countertrade
   b. Trade credit
   c. Buy-sell agreement
   d. 1990 Clean Air Act

Chapter 13. Sources of Financing: Debt and Equity

33. In microeconomics, industrial organization is the field which describes the behavior of firms in the marketplace with regard to production, pricing, employment and other decisions. _____ in this field range from classical issues such as opportunity cost to neoclassical concepts such as factors of production.

- Production theory basics
    - production efficiency
    - factors of production
    - total, average, and marginal product curves
    - marginal productivity
    - isoquants ' isocosts
    - the marginal rate of technical substitution
- Economic rent
    - classical factor rents
    - Paretian factor rents
- Production possibility frontier
    - what products are possible given a set of resources
    - the trade-off between producing one product rather than another
    - the marginal rate of transformation
- Production function
    - inputs
    - diminishing returns to inputs
    - the stages of production
    - shifts in a production function
- Cost theory
    - the different types of costs
        - opportunity cost
        - accounting cost or historical costs
        - transaction cost
        - sunk cost
        - marginal cost
    - the isocost line
- Cost-of-production theory of value
- Long-run cost and production functions
    - long-run average cost
    - long-run production function and efficiency
    - returns to scale and isoclines
    - minimum efficient scale
    - plant capacity
- Economies of density
- Economies of scale
    - the efficiency consequences of increasing or decreasing the level of production
- Economies of scope
    - the efficiency consequences of increasing or decreasing the number of different types of products produced, promoted, and distributed
- Optimum factor allocation
    - output elasticity of factor costs
    - marginal revenue product
    - marginal resource cost
- Pricing
    - various aspects of the pricing decision
- Transfer pricing
    - selling within a multi-divisional company
- Joint product pricing
    - price setting when two products are linked
- Price discrimination

- different prices to different buyers
- types of price discrimination
- yield management
- Price skimming
  - price discrimination over time
- Two part tariffs
  - charging a price composed of two parts, usually an initial fee and an ongoing fee
- Price points
  - the effects of a non-linear demand curve on pricing
- Cost-plus pricing
  - a markup is applied to a cost term in order to calculate price
  - cost-plus pricing with elasticity considerations
  - cost plus pricing is often used along with break even analysis
- Rate of return pricing
  - calculate price based on the required rate of return on investment, or rate of return on sales
- Profit maximization
  - determining the optimum price and quantity
  - the totals approach
  - marginal approach of production

Chapter 13. Sources of Financing: Debt and Equity

a. Pricing
b. Markup
c. Price floor
d. Topics

34. A _____ is typically described as a deliberate plan of action to guide decisions and achieve rational outcome(s.) However, the term may also be used to denote what is actually done, even though it is unplanned.

The term may apply to government, private sector organizations and groups, and individuals.

a. 33 Strategies of War
b. 1990 Clean Air Act
c. 28-hour day
d. Policy

35. A _____ is a funding round of securities which are sold without a initial public offering, usually to a small number of chosen private investors. In the United States, these placements are not subject to the Securities Act of 1933 and do not have to be registered with the Securities and Exchange Commission, although the sale must conform to SEC rules. _____s may typically consist of stocks, shares or warrants and purchasers are often institutional investors such as banks, insurance companies or pension funds.

a. Labor intensive
b. Niche market
c. Choquet integral
d. Private placement

36. _____ is an advertisement in which a particular product specifically mentions a competitor by name for the express purpose of showing why the competitor is inferior to the product naming it.

This should not be confused with parody advertisements, where a fictional product is being advertised for the purpose of poking fun at the particular advertisement, nor should it be confused with the use of a coined brand name for the purpose of comparing the product without actually naming an actual competitor. ('Wikipedia tastes better and is less filling than the Encyclopedia Galactica.')

In the 1980s, during what has been referred to as the cola wars, soft-drink manufacturer Pepsi ran a series of advertisements where people, caught on hidden camera, in a blind taste test, chose Pepsi over rival Coca-Cola.

a. 1990 Clean Air Act
b. 33 Strategies of War
c. 28-hour day
d. Comparative advertising

37. _____ is the process of sharing of skills, knowledge, technologies, methods of manufacturing, samples of manufacturing and facilities among governments and other institutions to ensure that scientific and technological developments are accessible to a wider range of users who can then further develop and exploit the technology into new products, processes, applications, materials or services. It is closely related to (and may arguably be considered a subset of) Knowledge transfer. Related terms, used almost synonymously, include 'technology valorisation' and 'technology commercialisation'.

a. Munn v. Illinois
b. Mediation
c. Competition law
d. Technology Transfer

38. The _____ is a United States government agency that provides support to small businesses.

The mission of the _____ is 'to maintain and strengthen the nation's economy by enabling the establishment and viability of small businesses and by assisting in the economic recovery of communities after disasters.'

The _____ makes loans directly to businesses and acts as a guarantor on bank loans. In some circumstances it also makes loans to victims of natural disasters, works to get government procurement contracts for small businesses, and assists businesses with management, technical and training issues.

- a. 28-hour day
- b. 1990 Clean Air Act
- c. 33 Strategies of War
- d. Small Business Administration

39. _____ is exchange of capital, goods, and services across international borders or territories. In most countries, it represents a significant share of gross domestic product (GDP.) While _____ has been present throughout much of history, its economic, social, and political importance has been on the rise in recent centuries.
- a. A4e
- b. AAAI
- c. International Trade
- d. A Stake in the Outcome

Chapter 14. Choosing the Right Location and Layout

1. _____ is, in very basic words, a position a firm occupies against its competitors.

According to Michael Porter, the three methods for creating a sustainable _____ are through:

1. Cost leadership

2. Differentiation

3. Focus (economics)

    a. 28-hour day   b. Competitive advantage
    c. Theory Z   d. 1990 Clean Air Act

2. _____ consists of the mental process of thinking involved with the process of judging the merits of multiple options and selecting one of them for action. Some simple examples include deciding whether to get up in the morning or go back to sleep, or selecting a given route for a journey. More complex examples (often decisions that affect what a person thinks or their core beliefs) include choosing a lifestyle, religious affiliation, or political position.

    a. Championship mobilization   b. Choice
    c. Trade study   d. Groups decision making

3. _____ or _____ data refers to selected population characteristics as used in government, marketing or opinion research, or the _____ profiles used in such research. Note the distinction from the term 'demography' Commonly-used _____s include race, age, income, disabilities, mobility (in terms of travel time to work or number of vehicles available), educational attainment, home ownership, employment status, and even location.

    a. Abraham Harold Maslow   b. Affiliation
    c. Adam Smith   d. Demographic

4. _____ is an integrated communications-based process through which individuals and communities discover that existing and newly-identified needs and wants may be satisfied by the products and services of others.

_____ is defined by the American _____ Association as the activity, set of institutions, and processes for creating, communicating, delivering, and exchanging offerings that have value for customers, clients, partners, and society at large. The term developed from the original meaning which referred literally to going to market, as in shopping, or going to a market to buy or sell goods or services.

    a. Customer relationship management   b. Marketing
    c. Market development   d. Disruptive technology

5. _____ , also referred to simply as a 'public offering' or 'flotation,' is when a company issues common stock or shares to the public for the first time. They are often issued by smaller, younger companies seeking capital to expand, but can also be done by large privately-owned companies looking to become publicly traded.

In an _____ the issuer may obtain the assistance of an underwriting firm, which helps it determine what type of security to issue (common or preferred), best offering price and time to bring it to market.

Chapter 14. Choosing the Right Location and Layout

a. Occupational Safety and Health Administration
b. Initial public offering
c. Outsourcing
d. Unemployment insurance

6. _____ is exchange of capital, goods, and services across international borders or territories. In most countries, it represents a significant share of gross domestic product (GDP.) While _____ has been present throughout much of history, its economic, social, and political importance has been on the rise in recent centuries.
   a. International Trade
   b. A4e
   c. A Stake in the Outcome
   d. AAAI

7. A _____ is a business that is privately owned and operated, with a small number of employees and relatively low volume of sales. The legal definition of 'small' often varies by country and industry, but is generally under 100 employees in the United States and under 50 employees in the European Union. In comparison, the definition of mid-sized business by the number of employees is generally under 500 in the U.S. and 250 for the European Union.
   a. Critical Success Factor
   b. Golden Boot Compensation
   c. Pre-determined overhead rate
   d. Small Business

8. _____ according to Onuoha (2007) is the practice of starting new organizations or revitalizing mature organizations, particularly new businesses generally in response to identified opportunities. _____ is often a difficult undertaking, as a vast majority of new businesses fail. Entrepreneurial activities are substantially different depending on the type of organization that is being started.
   a. AAAI
   b. A Stake in the Outcome
   c. A4e
   d. Entrepreneurship

9. In mainstream economic theories, the supply of labor is the number of total hours that workers wish to work at a given real wage rate. Realisticly, the _____ is a fuction of various factors within an economy. For instance, overpopulation increases the number of available workers driving down wages and can result in high unemployment.
   a. 28-hour day
   b. 1990 Clean Air Act
   c. 33 Strategies of War
   d. Labor supply

10. A _____ is a compensation, usually financial, received by a worker in exchange for their labor.

Compensation in terms of _____s is given to worker and compensation in terms of salary is given to employees. Compensation is a monetary benefits given to employees in returns of the services provided by them.

   a. Performance-related pay
   b. Profit-sharing agreement
   c. Wage
   d. State Compensation Insurance Fund

11. The _____ is a performance management tool for measuring whether the smaller-scale operational activities of a company are aligned with its larger-scale objectives in terms of vision and strategy.

By focusing not only on financial outcomes but also on the operational, marketing and developmental inputs to these, the _____ helps provide a more comprehensive view of a business, which in turn helps organizations act in their best long-term interests. This tool is also being used to address business response to climate change and greenhouse gas emissions.

Chapter 14. Choosing the Right Location and Layout   103

a. Commercial management
c. Middle management
b. Management development
d. Balanced scorecard

12. _____ is the state or fact of exclusive rights and control over property, which may be an object, land/real estate or intellectual property. An _____ right is also referred to as title. The concept of _____ has existed for thousands of years and in all cultures.

a. A4e
c. A Stake in the Outcome
b. Emanation of the state
d. Ownership

13. _____s are the recurring expenses which are related to the operation of a business -- or to the operation of a device, component, piece of equipment or facility.

For a commercial enterprise, _____s fall into two broad categories:

- fixed costs, which are the same whether the operation is closed or running at 100% capacity
- variable costs, which may increase depending on whether more production is done, and how it is done (producing 100 items of product might require 10 days of normal time or take 7 days if overtime is used. It may be more or less expensive to use overtime production depending on whether faster production means the product can be more profitable.)

Overhead costs for a business are the cost of resources used by an organization just to maintain its existence. Overhead costs are usually measured in monetary terms, but non-monetary overhead is possible in the form of time required to accomplish tasks.

Examples of overhead costs include:

- payment of rent on the office space a business occupies
- cost of electricity for the office lights
- some office personnel wages

Non-overhead costs are incremental costs, such as the cost of raw materials used in the goods a business sells.

In the case of a device, component, piece of equipment or facility (for the rest of this article, all of these items will be referred to in general as equipment), it is the regular, usual and customary recurring costs of operating the equipment.

a. Industrial market segmentation
c. Intangible assets
b. Operating cost
d. Induction programme

14. In economics, business, retail, and accounting, a _____ is the value of money that has been used up to produce something, and hence is not available for use anymore. In economics, a _____ is an alternative that is given up as a result of a decision. In business, the _____ may be one of acquisition, in which case the amount of money expended to acquire it is counted as _____.

Chapter 14. Choosing the Right Location and Layout

a. Cost overrun
c. Cost allocation
b. Fixed costs
d. Cost

15. Marketing research is a form of business research and is generally divided into two categories: consumer _____ and business-to-business (B2B) _____, which was previously known as industrial marketing research. Consumer marketing research studies the buying habits of individual people while business-to-business marketing research investigates the markets for products sold by one business to another.

Consumer _____ is a form of applied sociology that concentrates on understanding the behaviours, whims and preferences, of consumers in a market-based economy, and aims to understand the effects and comparative success of marketing campaigns.

a. Questionnaire
c. Mystery shoppers
b. Market research
d. Questionnaire construction

16. The term '_____' refers to the concept of collecting information and attempting to spot a pattern in the information. In some fields of study, the term '_____' has more formally-defined meanings.

In project management _____ is a mathematical technique that uses historical results to predict future outcome.

a. Regression analysis
c. Least squares
b. Trend analysis
d. Stepwise regression

17. _____ involves having senior executives periodically review their top executives and those in the next lower level to determine several backups for each senior position. This is important because it often takes years of grooming to develop effective senior managers. There is a critical shortage in companies of middle and top leaders for the next five years.

a. Kanban
c. Trademark
b. Risk management
d. Succession planning

18. A _____ is a form of partnership similar to a general partnership, except that in addition to one or more general partners (GPs), there are one or more limited partners (_____s.) It is a partnership in which only one partner is required to be a general partner.

The GPs are, in all major respects, in the same legal position as partners in a conventional firm, i.e. they have management control, share the right to use partnership property, share the profits of the firm in predefined proportions, and have joint and several liability for the debts of the partnership.

a. Growth capital
c. Pension fund
b. Private equity
d. Limited partnership

19. A _____ is a type of business entity in which partners (owners) share with each other the profits or losses of the business. _____s are often favored over corporations for taxation purposes, as the _____ structure does not generally incur a tax on profits before it is distributed to the partners (i.e. there is no dividend tax levied.) However, depending on the _____ structure and the jurisdiction in which it operates, owners of a _____ may be exposed to greater personal liability than they would as shareholders of a corporation.

Chapter 14. Choosing the Right Location and Layout

a. Due process
c. Mediation
b. Federal Employers Liability Act
d. Partnership

20. _____ is an advertisement in which a particular product specifically mentions a competitor by name for the express purpose of showing why the competitor is inferior to the product naming it.

This should not be confused with parody advertisements, where a fictional product is being advertised for the purpose of poking fun at the particular advertisement, nor should it be confused with the use of a coined brand name for the purpose of comparing the product without actually naming an actual competitor. ('Wikipedia tastes better and is less filling than the Encyclopedia Galactica.')

In the 1980s, during what has been referred to as the cola wars, soft-drink manufacturer Pepsi ran a series of advertisements where people, caught on hidden camera, in a blind taste test, chose Pepsi over rival Coca-Cola.

a. 1990 Clean Air Act
c. 33 Strategies of War
b. 28-hour day
d. Comparative advertising

21. The phrase mergers and _____s refers to the aspect of corporate strategy, corporate finance and management dealing with the buying, selling and combining of different companies that can aid, finance, or help a growing company in a given industry grow rapidly without having to create another business entity.

An _____, also known as a takeover or a buyout, is the buying of one company (the 'target') by another. An _____ may be friendly or hostile.

a. A4e
c. AAAI
b. A Stake in the Outcome
d. Acquisition

22. _____, commonly known as e-commerce, consists of the buying and selling of products or services over electronic systems such as the Internet and other computer networks. The amount of trade conducted electronically has grown extraordinarily with widespread Internet usage. The use of commerce is conducted in this way, spurring and drawing on innovations in electronic funds transfer, supply chain management, Internet marketing, online transaction processing, electronic data interchange (EDI), inventory management systems, and automated data collection systems.

a. Electronic Commerce
c. A Stake in the Outcome
b. A4e
d. Online shopping

23. A _____ is a professional who provides advice in a particular area of expertise such as management, accountancy, the environment, entertainment, technology, law , human resources, marketing, medicine, finance, economics, public affairs, communication, engineering, sound system design, graphic design, or waste management.

A _____ is usually an expert or a professional in a specific field and has a wide knowledge of the subject matter. A _____ usually works for a consultancy firm or is self-employed, and engages with multiple and changing clients.

a. 33 Strategies of War
c. 1990 Clean Air Act
b. 28-hour day
d. Consultant

Chapter 14. Choosing the Right Location and Layout

24. _____ is one of the four elements of marketing mix. An organization or set of organizations (go-betweens) involved in the process of making a product or service available for use or consumption by a consumer or business user.

The other three parts of the marketing mix are product, pricing, and promotion.

 a. Job creation programs
 b. Distribution
 c. Missing completely at random
 d. Matching theory

25. The _____ of 1990 (ADA) is the short title of United States (Pub.L. 101-336, 104 Stat. 327, enacted July 26, 1990), codified at 42 U.S.C. § 12101 et seq. It was signed into law on July 26, 1990, by President George H. W. Bush, and later amended with changes effective January 1, 2009. The ADA is a wide-ranging civil rights law that prohibits, under certain circumstances, discrimination based on disability. It affords similar protections against discrimination to Americans with disabilities as the Civil Rights Act of 1964,

 a. Equal Pay Act of 1963
 b. Australian labour law
 c. Americans with Disabilities Act
 d. Employment discrimination

26. _____ is a medical condition in which the median nerve is compressed at the wrist, leading to paresthesias, numbness and muscle weakness in the hand. The diagnosis of _____ is often misapplied to patients who have activity-related arm pain.

Most cases of _____ are idiopathic (without known cause); genetic factors determine most of the risk, and the role of arm use and other environmental factors is disputed.

 a. 1990 Clean Air Act
 b. 28-hour day
 c. 33 Strategies of War
 d. Carpal tunnel syndrome

27. _____s is the science of designing the job, equipment, and workplace to fit the worker. Proper _____ design is necessary to prevent repetitive strain injuries, which can develop over time and can lead to long-term disability.

_____s is concerned with the 'fit' between people and their work.

 a. A4e
 b. A Stake in the Outcome
 c. AAAI
 d. Ergonomic

28. _____ generally refers to a list of all planned expenses and revenues. It is a plan for saving and spending. A _____ is an important concept in microeconomics, which uses a _____ line to illustrate the trade-offs between two or more goods.

 a. 28-hour day
 b. 1990 Clean Air Act
 c. Budget
 d. 33 Strategies of War

29. A _____ is a formal statement of a set of business goals, the reasons why they are believed attainable, and the plan for reaching those goals. It may also contain background information about the organization or team attempting to reach those goals.

The business goals may be defined for for-profit or for non-profit organizations.

a. Crisis management
b. Distributed management
c. Time management
d. Business plan

Chapter 15. Global Aspects of Entrepreneurship

1. _____ according to Onuoha (2007) is the practice of starting new organizations or revitalizing mature organizations, particularly new businesses generally in response to identified opportunities. _____ is often a difficult undertaking, as a vast majority of new businesses fail. Entrepreneurial activities are substantially different depending on the type of organization that is being started.
   a. Entrepreneurship
   b. A Stake in the Outcome
   c. AAAI
   d. A4e

2. _____ is a dynamic of being mutually and physically responsible to and sharing a common set of principles with others. This concept differs distinctly from 'dependence' in that an interdependent relationship implies that all participants are emotionally, economically, ecologically and or morally 'interdependent.' Some people advocate freedom or independence as a sort of ultimate good; others do the same with devotion to one's family, community, or society. _____ recognizes the truth in each position and weaves them together.
   a. A Stake in the Outcome
   b. Interdependence
   c. A4e
   d. AAAI

3. _____ generally refers to a list of all planned expenses and revenues. It is a plan for saving and spending. A _____ is an important concept in microeconomics, which uses a _____ line to illustrate the trade-offs between two or more goods.
   a. 1990 Clean Air Act
   b. 33 Strategies of War
   c. 28-hour day
   d. Budget

4. A _____ is a formal statement of a set of business goals, the reasons why they are believed attainable, and the plan for reaching those goals. It may also contain background information about the organization or team attempting to reach those goals.

The business goals may be defined for for-profit or for non-profit organizations.

   a. Business plan
   b. Distributed management
   c. Time management
   d. Crisis management

5. In economics, business, retail, and accounting, a _____ is the value of money that has been used up to produce something, and hence is not available for use anymore. In economics, a _____ is an alternative that is given up as a result of a decision. In business, the _____ may be one of acquisition, in which case the amount of money expended to acquire it is counted as _____.
   a. Cost allocation
   b. Cost
   c. Cost overrun
   d. Fixed costs

6. The concept of quality costs is a means to quantify the total _____-related efforts and deficiencies. It was first described by Armand V. Feigenbaum in a 1956 Harvard Business Review article.

Prior to its introduction, the general perception was that higher quality requires higher costs, either by buying better materials or machines or by hiring more labor.

   a. Cost accounting
   b. Fixed costs
   c. Cost of quality
   d. Quality costs

Chapter 15. Global Aspects of Entrepreneurship

7. _____ is one of the four elements of marketing mix. An organization or set of organizations (go-betweens) involved in the process of making a product or service available for use or consumption by a consumer or business user.

The other three parts of the marketing mix are product, pricing, and promotion.

   a. Matching theory
   b. Missing completely at random
   c. Job creation programs
   d. Distribution

8. The phrase mergers and _____s refers to the aspect of corporate strategy, corporate finance and management dealing with the buying, selling and combining of different companies that can aid, finance, or help a growing company in a given industry grow rapidly without having to create another business entity.

An _____, also known as a takeover or a buyout, is the buying of one company (the 'target') by another. An _____ may be friendly or hostile.

   a. A Stake in the Outcome
   b. AAAI
   c. A4e
   d. Acquisition

9. _____, commonly known as e-commerce, consists of the buying and selling of products or services over electronic systems such as the Internet and other computer networks. The amount of trade conducted electronically has grown extraordinarily with widespread Internet usage. The use of commerce is conducted in this way, spurring and drawing on innovations in electronic funds transfer, supply chain management, Internet marketing, online transaction processing, electronic data interchange (EDI), inventory management systems, and automated data collection systems.
   a. A4e
   b. A Stake in the Outcome
   c. Electronic Commerce
   d. Online shopping

10. _____ is the state or fact of exclusive rights and control over property, which may be an object, land/real estate or intellectual property. An _____ right is also referred to as title. The concept of _____ has existed for thousands of years and in all cultures.
    a. A Stake in the Outcome
    b. Emanation of the state
    c. Ownership
    d. A4e

11. _____ is an organization's process of defining its strategy and making decisions on allocating its resources to pursue this strategy, including its capital and people. Various business analysis techniques can be used in _____, including SWOT analysis (Strengths, Weaknesses, Opportunities, and Threats) and PEST analysis (Political, Economic, Social, and Technological analysis) or STEER analysis involving Socio-cultural, Technological, Economic, Ecological, and Regulatory factors and EPISTEL (Environment, Political, Informatic, Social, Technological, Economic and Legal).

_____ is the formal consideration of an organization's future course. All _____ deals with at least one of three key questions:

   1. 'What do we do?'
   2. 'For whom do we do it?'
   3. 'How do we excel?'

Chapter 15. Global Aspects of Entrepreneurship

In business _____, the third question is better phrased 'How can we beat or avoid competition?'. (Bradford and Duncan, page 1.)

a. 28-hour day
b. 33 Strategies of War
c. 1990 Clean Air Act
d. Strategic planning

12. An _____ is the impact an individual, business, organization or corporation has on the World Wide Web and, practicably, the traceable residue that it leaves behind through this interaction.

_____s are starting to be used to supplement interviews by some 'to research potential employees by examining what they find on the Internet.'

It also aids Law Enforcement by enabling them to get information that would be unavailable otherwise due to a lack of probable cause. More recently, with the increasing amount of data being stored on the internet it is possible to find information on someone using their Cyber Shadow/Digital Shadow.

a. AAAI
b. A Stake in the Outcome
c. A4e
d. Internet footprint

13. Marketing research is a form of business research and is generally divided into two categories: consumer _____ and business-to-business (B2B) _____, which was previously known as industrial marketing research. Consumer marketing research studies the buying habits of individual people while business-to-business marketing research investigates the markets for products sold by one business to another.

Consumer _____ is a form of applied sociology that concentrates on understanding the behaviours, whims and preferences, of consumers in a market-based economy, and aims to understand the effects and comparative success of marketing campaigns.

a. Questionnaire
b. Questionnaire construction
c. Mystery shoppers
d. Market research

14. A _____ is a professional who provides advice in a particular area of expertise such as management, accountancy, the environment, entertainment, technology, law , human resources, marketing, medicine, finance, economics, public affairs, communication, engineering, sound system design, graphic design, or waste management.

A _____ is usually an expert or a professional in a specific field and has a wide knowledge of the subject matter. A _____ usually works for a consultancy firm or is self-employed, and engages with multiple and changing clients.

a. 28-hour day
b. 33 Strategies of War
c. 1990 Clean Air Act
d. Consultant

Chapter 15. Global Aspects of Entrepreneurship

15. A _____ is an entity formed between two or more parties to undertake economic activity together. The parties agree to create a new entity by both contributing equity, and they then share in the revenues, expenses, and control of the enterprise. The venture can be for one specific project only, or a continuing business relationship such as the Fuji Xerox _____.
    a. Patent
    b. Civil Rights Act of 1991
    c. Joint venture
    d. Meritor Savings Bank v. Vinson

16. An _____ is a person who has possession of an enterprise and assumes significant accountability for the inherent risks and the outcome. It is an ambitious leader who combines land, labor, and capital to create and market new goods or services. The term is a loanword from French and was first defined by the Irish economist Richard Cantillon.
    a. AAAI
    b. A Stake in the Outcome
    c. A4e
    d. Entrepreneur

17. _____ refers to the methods of practicing and using another person's business philosophy. The franchisor grants the independent operator the right to distribute its products, techniques, and trademarks for a percentage of gross monthly sales and a royalty fee. Various tangibles and intangibles such as national or international advertising, training, and other support services are commonly made available by the franchisor.
    a. ServiceMaster
    b. 28-hour day
    c. Franchising
    d. 1990 Clean Air Act

18. _____ is exchange of capital, goods, and services across international borders or territories. In most countries, it represents a significant share of gross domestic product (GDP.) While _____ has been present throughout much of history, its economic, social, and political importance has been on the rise in recent centuries.
    a. International trade
    b. A Stake in the Outcome
    c. AAAI
    d. A4e

19. _____ is an integrated communications-based process through which individuals and communities discover that existing and newly-identified needs and wants may be satisfied by the products and services of others.

    _____ is defined by the American _____ Association as the activity, set of institutions, and processes for creating, communicating, delivering, and exchanging offerings that have value for customers, clients, partners, and society at large. The term developed from the original meaning which referred literally to going to market, as in shopping, or going to a market to buy or sell goods or services.

    a. Market development
    b. Disruptive technology
    c. Customer relationship management
    d. Marketing

20. A _____ is a written document that details the necessary actions to achieve one or more marketing objectives. It can be for a product or service, a brand, or a product line. _____s cover between one and five years.
    a. Marketing strategy
    b. Market development
    c. Disruptive technology
    d. Marketing plan

21. _____ is an international trip by government officials and businesspeople that is organized by agencies of national of provincial governments for purpose of exploring international business opportunities. Business people who attend _____s are typically introduced both to important business contacts and to well-placed government officials.

Chapter 15. Global Aspects of Entrepreneurship

a. Trade mission
b. 33 Strategies of War
c. 28-hour day
d. 1990 Clean Air Act

22. The _____ is a performance management tool for measuring whether the smaller-scale operational activities of a company are aligned with its larger-scale objectives in terms of vision and strategy.

By focusing not only on financial outcomes but also on the operational, marketing and developmental inputs to these, the _____ helps provide a more comprehensive view of a business, which in turn helps organizations act in their best long-term interests. This tool is also being used to address business response to climate change and greenhouse gas emissions.

a. Commercial management
b. Management development
c. Middle management
d. Balanced scorecard

23. A standard, commercial _____ is a document issued mostly by a financial institution, used primarily in trade finance, which usually provides an irrevocable payment undertaking.

The LC can also be the source of payment for a traction, meaning that redeeming the _____ will pay an exporter. Letters of credit are used primarily in international trade transactions of significant value, for deals between a supplier in one country and a customer in another.

a. Sarbanes-Oxley Act of 2002
b. Letter of credit
c. Diminishing returns
d. False Claims Act

24. The _____ of 1977 (15 U.S.C. §§ 78dd-1, et seq.) is a United States federal law known primarily for two of its main provisions, one that addresses accounting transparency requirements under the Securities Exchange Act of 1934 and another concerning bribery of foreign officials.

a. Limited liability
b. Social Security Act of 1965
c. Meritor Savings Bank v. Vinson
d. Foreign Corrupt Practices Act

25. _____ , also referred to simply as a 'public offering' or 'flotation,' is when a company issues common stock or shares to the public for the first time. They are often issued by smaller, younger companies seeking capital to expand, but can also be done by large privately-owned companies looking to become publicly traded.

In an _____ the issuer may obtain the assistance of an underwriting firm, which helps it determine what type of security to issue (common or preferred), best offering price and time to bring it to market.

a. Occupational Safety and Health Administration
b. Unemployment insurance
c. Outsourcing
d. Initial public offering

26. _____ is subcontracting a process, such as product design or manufacturing, to a third-party company. The decision to outsource is often made in the interest of lowering cost or making better use of time and energy costs, redirecting or conserving energy directed at the competencies of a particular business, or to make more efficient use of land, labor, capital, (information) technology and resources. _____ became part of the business lexicon during the 1980s.

a. Unemployment insurance
b. Outsourcing
c. Operant conditioning
d. Opinion leadership

27. _____ are legal property rights over creations of the mind, both artistic and commercial, and the corresponding fields of law. Under _____ law, owners are granted certain exclusive rights to a variety of intangible assets, such as musical, literary, and artistic works; ideas, discoveries and inventions; and words, phrases, symbols, and designs. Common types of _____ include copyrights, trademarks, patents, industrial design rights and trade secrets.

a. Unemployment Action Center
b. Intent
c. Equal Pay Act
d. Intellectual property

28. _____ plant, and equipment, is a term used in accountancy for assets and property which cannot easily be converted into cash. This can be compared with current assets such as cash or bank accounts, which are described as liquid assets. In most cases, only tangible assets are referred to as fixed.

a. 1990 Clean Air Act
b. 28-hour day
c. 33 Strategies of War
d. Fixed asset

29. _____ is a form of marketing developed from direct response marketing campaigns conducted in the 1970s and 1980s which emphasizes customer retention and satisfaction, rather than a dominant focus on point-of-sale transactions.

_____ differs from other forms of marketing in that it recognizes the long term value to the firm of keeping customers, as opposed to direct or 'Intrusion' marketing, which focuses upon acquisition of new clients by targeting majority demographics based upon prospective client lists.

_____ refers to a long-term and mutually beneficial arrangement wherein both the buyer and seller focus on value enhancement with the goal of providing a more satisfying exchange.

a. 28-hour day
b. Relationship marketing
c. Guerrilla marketing
d. 1990 Clean Air Act

30. A _____ is a general term that describes any government policy or regulation that restricts international trade. The barriers can take many forms, including the following terms that include many restrictions in international trade within multiple countries that import and export any items of trade.

- Import duty
- Import licenses
- Export licenses
- Import quotas
- Tariffs
- Subsidies
- Non-tariff barriers to trade
- Voluntary Export Restraints
- Local Content Requirements
- Embargo

Most _____s work on the same principle: the imposition of some sort of cost on trade that raises the price of the traded products. If two or more nations repeatedly use _____s against each other, then a trade war results.

a. Trade creation
b. Customs brokerage
c. Most favoured nation
d. Trade Barrier

31. The _____ is an international organization designed by its founders to supervise and liberalize international trade. The organization officially commenced on 1 January 1995, under the Marrakesh Agreement, succeeding the 1947 General Agreement on Tariffs and Trade (GATT.)

The _____ deals with regulation of trade between participating countries; it provides a framework for negotiating and formalising trade agreements, and a dispute resolution process aimed at enforcing participants' adherence to _____ agreements which are signed by representatives of member governments and ratified by their parliaments.

a. Network planning and design
b. 1990 Clean Air Act
c. National Institute for Occupational Safety and Health
d. World Trade Organization

32. _____ is a type of trade policy that allows traders to act and transact without interference from government. Thus, the policy permits trading partners mutual gains from trade, with goods and services produced according to the theory of comparative advantage.

Under a _____ policy, prices are a reflection of true supply and demand, and are the sole determinant of resource allocation.

a. Free Trade
b. 28-hour day
c. 1990 Clean Air Act
d. 33 Strategies of War

33. _____ is a designated group of countries that have agreed to eliminate tariffs, quotas and preferences on most (if not all) goods and services traded between them. It can be considered the second stage of economic integration. Countries choose this kind of economic integration form if their economical structures are complementary.

a. 33 Strategies of War
b. Free trade area
c. 1990 Clean Air Act
d. 28-hour day

34. The _____ is a trilateral trade bloc in North America created by the governments of the United States, Canada, and Mexico. The agreement creating the trade bloc came into force on January 1, 1994. It superseded the Canada-United States Free Trade Agreement between the U.S. and Canada.

a. Career portfolios
b. Business war game
c. Trade union
d. North American Free Trade Agreement

Chapter 16. Building a New Venture Team and Planning for the Next Generation

1. _____ has been described as the 'process of social influence in which one person can enlist the aid and support of others in the accomplishment of a common task' . A definition more inclusive of followers comes from Alan Keith of Genentech who said '_____ is ultimately about creating a way for people to contribute to making something extraordinary happen.'

_____ is one of the most salient aspects of the organizational context. However, defining _____ has been challenging.

   a. Situational leadership
   b. Leadership
   c. 28-hour day
   d. 1990 Clean Air Act

2. _____ is a process and a set of procedures used to estimate the economic value of an owner's interest in a business. Valuation is used by financial market participants to determine the price they are willing to pay or receive to consummate a sale of a business. In addition to estimating the selling price of a business, the same valuation tools are often used by business appraisers to resolve disputes related to estate and gift taxation, divorce litigation, allocate business purchase price among business assets, establish a formula for estimating the value of partners' ownership interest for buy-sell agreements, and many other business and legal purposes.

   a. Robinson-Patman Act
   b. No-FEAR Act
   c. Munn v. Illinois
   d. Business valuation

3. _____ is the state or fact of exclusive rights and control over property, which may be an object, land/real estate or intellectual property. An _____ right is also referred to as title. The concept of _____ has existed for thousands of years and in all cultures.

   a. Emanation of the state
   b. A Stake in the Outcome
   c. A4e
   d. Ownership

4. _____ , also referred to simply as a 'public offering' or 'flotation,' is when a company issues common stock or shares to the public for the first time. They are often issued by smaller, younger companies seeking capital to expand, but can also be done by large privately-owned companies looking to become publicly traded.

In an _____ the issuer may obtain the assistance of an underwriting firm, which helps it determine what type of security to issue (common or preferred), best offering price and time to bring it to market.

   a. Occupational Safety and Health Administration
   b. Initial public offering
   c. Outsourcing
   d. Unemployment insurance

5. The 'business case for _____', theorizes that in a global marketplace, a company that employs a diverse workforce (both men and women, people of many generations, people from ethnically and racially diverse backgrounds etc.) is better able to understand the demographics of the marketplace it serves and is thus better equipped to thrive in that marketplace than a company that has a more limited range of employee demographics.

An additional corollary suggests that a company that supports the _____ of its workforce can also improve employee satisfaction, productivity and retention.

   a. Kanban
   b. Virtual team
   c. Trademark
   d. Diversity

Chapter 16. Building a New Venture Team and Planning for the Next Generation

6. The _____ is the labour pool in employment. It is generally used to describe those working for a single company or industry, but can also apply to a geographic region like a city, country, state, etc. The term generally excludes the employers or management, and implies those involved in manual labour.
   a. Workforce
   b. Division of labour
   c. Work-life balance
   d. Pink-collar worker

7. In decision theory and estimation theory, the _____ of an estimator, $\hat{\theta}$, of an unknown parameter of the distribution, θ, is the expected value of the loss function

$$R(\theta, \hat{\theta}) = \mathbb{E}_\theta L(\theta, \hat{\theta}) = \int L(\theta, \hat{\theta}) \, dP_\theta.$$

where dP_θ is a probability measure parametrized by θ.

- For a scalar parameter θ and a quadratic loss function,

$$L(\theta, \hat{\theta}) = (\theta - \hat{\theta})^2$$

the _____ function becomes the mean squared error of the estimate,

$$R(\theta, \hat{\theta}) = E_\theta (\theta - \hat{\theta})^2$$

- In density estimation, the unknown parameter is probability density itself. The loss function is typically chosen to be a norm in an appropriate function space. For example, for L^2 norm,

$$L(f, \hat{f}) = \|f - \hat{f}\|_2^2$$

the _____ function becomes the mean integrated squared error

$$R(f, \hat{f}) = E\|f - \hat{f}\|^2$$

   a. Risk aversion
   b. Financial modeling
   c. Linear model
   d. Risk

8. _____ according to Onuoha (2007) is the practice of starting new organizations or revitalizing mature organizations, particularly new businesses generally in response to identified opportunities. _____ is often a difficult undertaking, as a vast majority of new businesses fail. Entrepreneurial activities are substantially different depending on the type of organization that is being started.
   a. A4e
   b. A Stake in the Outcome
   c. AAAI
   d. Entrepreneurship

9. _____ or _____ data refers to selected population characteristics as used in government, marketing or opinion research, or the _____ profiles used in such research. Note the distinction from the term 'demography' Commonly-used _____s include race, age, income, disabilities, mobility (in terms of travel time to work or number of vehicles available), educational attainment, home ownership, employment status, and even location.
   a. Demographic
   b. Adam Smith
   c. Affiliation
   d. Abraham Harold Maslow

10. In economics, business, retail, and accounting, a _____ is the value of money that has been used up to produce something, and hence is not available for use anymore. In economics, a _____ is an alternative that is given up as a result of a decision. In business, the _____ may be one of acquisition, in which case the amount of money expended to acquire it is counted as _____.
    a. Cost
    b. Fixed costs
    c. Cost overrun
    d. Cost allocation

11. _____ is a contract between two parties, one being the employer and the other being the employee. An employee may be defined as: 'A person in the service of another under any contract of hire, express or implied, oral or written, where the employer has the power or right to control and direct the employee in the material details of how the work is to be performed.' Black's Law Dictionary page 471 (5th ed. 1979.)
    a. Exit interview
    b. Employment counsellor
    c. Employment rate
    d. Employment

12. _____ is a form of communication that typically attempts to persuade potential customers to purchase or to consume more of a particular brand of product or service. 'While now central to the contemporary global economy and the reproduction of global production networks, it is only quite recently that _____ has been more than a marginal influence on patterns of sales and production. The formation of modern _____ was intimately bound up with the emergence of new forms of monopoly capitalism around the end of the 19th and beginning of the 20th century as one element in corporate strategies to create, organize and where possible control markets, especially for mass produced consumer goods.
    a. A4e
    b. Advertising
    c. AAAI
    d. A Stake in the Outcome

13. _____ is an organization's process of defining its strategy and making decisions on allocating its resources to pursue this strategy, including its capital and people. Various business analysis techniques can be used in _____, including SWOT analysis (Strengths, Weaknesses, Opportunities, and Threats) and PEST analysis (Political, Economic, Social, and Technological analysis) or STEER analysis involving Socio-cultural, Technological, Economic, Ecological, and Regulatory factors and EPISTEL (Environment, Political, Informatic, Social, Technological, Economic and Legal)

_____ is the formal consideration of an organization's future course. All _____ deals with at least one of three key questions:

1. 'What do we do?'
2. 'For whom do we do it?'
3. 'How do we excel?'

In business _____, the third question is better phrased 'How can we beat or avoid competition?'. (Bradford and Duncan, page 1.)

Chapter 16. Building a New Venture Team and Planning for the Next Generation

a. 1990 Clean Air Act
b. 28-hour day
c. Strategic planning
d. 33 Strategies of War

14. _____, commonly known as e-commerce, consists of the buying and selling of products or services over electronic systems such as the Internet and other computer networks. The amount of trade conducted electronically has grown extraordinarily with widespread Internet usage. The use of commerce is conducted in this way, spurring and drawing on innovations in electronic funds transfer, supply chain management, Internet marketing, online transaction processing, electronic data interchange (EDI), inventory management systems, and automated data collection systems.

a. Online shopping
b. A Stake in the Outcome
c. Electronic Commerce
d. A4e

15. _____ is an internal recruitment method employed by organisations to identify potential candidates from their existing employees social networks. An _____ scheme encourages a company's existing employees to select and recruit the suitable candidates from their social networks. As a reward, the employer typically pays the referring employee a referral bonus.

a. Employment agency
b. Internet recruiting
c. Executive search
d. Employee referral

16. _____ consists of the mental process of thinking involved with the process of judging the merits of multiple options and selecting one of them for action. Some simple examples include deciding whether to get up in the morning or go back to sleep, or selecting a given route for a journey. More complex examples (often decisions that affect what a person thinks or their core beliefs) include choosing a lifestyle, religious affiliation, or political position.

a. Championship mobilization
b. Groups decision making
c. Trade study
d. Choice

17. The _____, commonly known as the DOT was the creation of the U.S. Employment Service, which used its thousands of occupational definitions to match job seekers to jobs from 1939 to the late 1990s.

Before 1939, nationwide occupational information was not conveniently reported by the Employment Service. By 1939, it had become clear to the Employment service that a standardized volume of job definitions was needed for employment-related purposes.

a. 33 Strategies of War
b. 28-hour day
c. 1990 Clean Air Act
d. Dictionary of Occupational Titles

18. _____ refers to various methodologies for analyzing the requirements of a job.

The general purpose of _____ is to document the requirements of a job and the work performed. Job and task analysis is performed as a basis for later improvements, including: definition of a job domain; describing a job; developing performance appraisals, selection systems, promotion criteria, training needs assessment, and compensation plans.

a. Hersey-Blanchard situational theory
b. Management process
c. Work design
d. Job analysis

Chapter 16. Building a New Venture Team and Planning for the Next Generation   119

19. A _____ is a list of the general tasks and responsibilities of a position. Typically, it also includes to whom the position reports, specifications such as the qualifications needed by the person in the job, salary range for the position, etc. A _____ is usually developed by conducting a job analysis, which includes examining the tasks and sequences of tasks necessary to perform the job.

   a. Recruitment Process Insourcing
   b. Recruitment
   c. Recruitment advertising
   d. Job description

20. _____ is the act of scouring the internet to locate both actively-searching job seekers and also individuals who are content in their current position (these are called 'passive candidates'.) It is a field of dramatic growth and constant change that has given birth to a dynamic multi billion dollar industry.

Traditionally, recruiters use large job boards, niche job boards, as well as social and business networking to locate these individuals.

   a. Employment agency
   b. Employee referral
   c. Executive search
   d. Internet recruiting

21. A _____ is a formal statement of a set of business goals, the reasons why they are believed attainable, and the plan for reaching those goals. It may also contain background information about the organization or team attempting to reach those goals.

The business goals may be defined for for-profit or for non-profit organizations.

   a. Time management
   b. Crisis management
   c. Distributed management
   d. Business plan

22. A _____ or background investigation is the process of looking up and compiling criminal records, commercial records and financial records (in certain instances such as employment screening) of an individual.

_____s are often requested by employers on job candidates, especially on candidates seeking a position that requires high security or a position of trust, such as in a school, hospital, financial institution, airport, and government (including law enforcement and military.) These checks are traditionally administered by a government agency for a nominal fee, but can also be administered by private companies.

   a. Labour productivity
   b. Time and attendance
   c. Malcolm Baldrige National Quality Award
   d. Background check

23. _____ generally refers to a list of all planned expenses and revenues. It is a plan for saving and spending. A _____ is an important concept in microeconomics, which uses a _____ line to illustrate the trade-offs between two or more goods.

   a. 1990 Clean Air Act
   b. 33 Strategies of War
   c. 28-hour day
   d. Budget

Chapter 16. Building a New Venture Team and Planning for the Next Generation

24. _____ is a term used for a number of concepts involving either the performance of an investigation of a business or person, or the performance of an act with a certain standard of care. It can be a legal obligation, but the term will more commonly apply to voluntary investigations. A common example of _____ in various industries is the process through which a potential acquirer evaluates a target company or its assets for acquisition.

   a. Flextime
   b. Due diligence
   c. Negligence in employment
   d. Technology transfer

25. A _____ is a process in which a potential employee is evaluated by an employer for prospective employment in their company, organization and was established in the late 16th century.

   A _____ typically precedes the hiring decision, and is used to evaluate the candidate. The interview is usually preceded by the evaluation of submitted résumés from interested candidates, then selecting a small number of candidates for interviews.

   a. Job interview
   b. Split shift
   c. Supported employment
   d. Payrolling

26. A _____ is a professional who provides advice in a particular area of expertise such as management, accountancy, the environment, entertainment, technology, law , human resources, marketing, medicine, finance, economics, public affairs, communication, engineering, sound system design, graphic design, or waste management.

   A _____ is usually an expert or a professional in a specific field and has a wide knowledge of the subject matter. A _____ usually works for a consultancy firm or is self-employed, and engages with multiple and changing clients.

   a. 1990 Clean Air Act
   b. Consultant
   c. 33 Strategies of War
   d. 28-hour day

27. _____ is an idea in the field of Organizational studies and management which describes the psychology, attitudes, experiences, beliefs and Values (personal and cultural values) of an organization. It has been defined as 'the specific collection of values and norms that are shared by people and groups in an organization and that control the way they interact with each other and with stakeholders outside the organization.'

   This definition continues to explain organizational values also known as 'beliefs and ideas about what kinds of goals members of an organization should pursue and ideas about the appropriate kinds or standards of behavior organizational members should use to achieve these goals. From organizational values develop organizational norms, guidelines or expectations that prescribe appropriate kinds of behavior by employees in particular situations and control the behavior of organizational members towards one another.'

   _____ is not the same as corporate culture.

   a. Union shop
   b. Organizational development
   c. Organizational effectiveness
   d. Organizational culture

Chapter 16. Building a New Venture Team and Planning for the Next Generation

28. An _____ is a person who has possession of an enterprise and assumes significant accountability for the inherent risks and the outcome. It is an ambitious leader who combines land, labor, and capital to create and market new goods or services. The term is a loanword from French and was first defined by the Irish economist Richard Cantillon.

   a. A Stake in the Outcome   b. AAAI
   c. A4e   d. Entrepreneur

29. _____, commonly abbreviated to Gen X, is a term used to refer to a generational cohort of children born after the baby boom ended and usually prior to the 1980s

The term _____ has been used in demography, the social sciences, and marketing, though it is most often used in popular culture.

In the U.S. _____ was originally referred to as the 'baby bust' generation because of the drop in the birth rate following the baby boom.

   a. Affiliation   b. Adam Smith
   c. Abraham Harold Maslow   d. Generation X

30. _____ means increasing the scope of a job through extending the range of its job duties and responsibilities. This contradicts the principles of specialisation and the division of labour whereby work is divided into small units, each of which is performed repetitively by an individual worker. Some motivational theories suggest that the boredom and alienation caused by the division of labour can actually cause efficiency to fall.

   a. Centralization   b. Job enlargement
   c. Mock interview   d. Delayering

31. _____ is an approach to management development where an individual is moved through a schedule of assignments designed to give him or her a breadth of exposure to the entire operation.

_____ is also practiced to allow qualified employees to gain more insights into the processes of a company, and to reduce boredom and increase job satisfaction through job variation.

The term _____ can also mean the scheduled exchange of persons in offices, especially in public offices, prior to the end of incumbency or the legislative period.

   a. 28-hour day   b. 1990 Clean Air Act
   c. 33 Strategies of War   d. Job rotation

32. In mathematical logic, _____ is a valid argument and rule of inference which makes the inference that, if the conjunction A and B is true, then A is true, and B is true.

In formal language:

$$A \wedge B \vdash A$$

or

$$A \wedge B \vdash B$$

The argument has one premise, namely a conjunction, and one often uses _____ in longer arguments to derive one of the conjuncts.

An example in English:

It's raining and it's pouring.

a. Validity
c. 1990 Clean Air Act
b. Fuzzy logic
d. Simplification

33. _____ describes the situation when output from (or information about the result of) an event or phenomenon in the past will influence the same event/phenomenon in the present or future. When an event is part of a chain of cause-and-effect that forms a circuit or loop, then the event is said to 'feed back' into itself.

_____ is also a synonym for:

- _____ signal; the information about the initial event that is the basis for subsequent modification of the event.
- _____ loop; the causal path that leads from the initial generation of the _____ signal to the subsequent modification of the event.

_____ is a mechanism, process or signal that is looped back to control a system within itself. Such a loop is called a _____ loop.

a. Feedback
c. Feedback loop
b. 1990 Clean Air Act
d. Positive feedback

34. _____ is a variable work schedule, in contrast to traditional work arrangements requiring employees to work a standard 9am to 5pm day. Under _____, there is typically a core period of the day when employees are expected to be at work (for example, between 11 am and 3pm), while the rest of the working day is 'flexitime', in which employees can choose when they work, subject to achieving total daily, weekly or monthly hours in the region of what the employer expects, and subject to the necessary work being done.

A _____ policy allows staff to determine when they will work, while a flexplace policy allows staff to determine where they will work.

a. Flextime
c. Certificate of Incorporation
b. Bennett Amendment
d. Fiduciary

Chapter 16. Building a New Venture Team and Planning for the Next Generation

35. _____ is an attempt to motivate employees by giving them the opportunity to use the range of their abilities. It is an idea that was developed by the American psychologist Frederick Herzberg in the 1950s. It can be contrasted to job enlargement which simply increases the number of tasks without changing the challenge.

   a. Catfish effect
   b. Cash cow
   c. C-A-K-E
   d. Job enrichment

36. _____ is a company policy or program that enables employees to have more decision authority on where they will work regardless of time of day. For example, they may choose to work in the office or from home or from a client's office or even a caf>é.

   a. Flexplace
   b. 28-hour day
   c. 33 Strategies of War
   d. 1990 Clean Air Act

37. _____, e-commuting, e-work, telework, working from home (WFH), or working at home (WAH) is a work arrangement in which employees enjoy flexibility in working location and hours. In other words, the daily commute to a central place of work is replaced by telecommunication links. Many work from home, while others, occasionally also referred to as nomad workers or web commuters utilize mobile telecommunications technology to work from coffee shops or myriad other locations.

   a. Telecommuting
   b. 1990 Clean Air Act
   c. 33 Strategies of War
   d. 28-hour day

38. _____ originates from the definition of being the temporary physical occupant of a work station or surface by a particular employee. The term _____ is thought to be derived from the naval practice, called hot racking, where sailors on different shifts share bunks. Originating as a trend in the late 1980s-early 1990s, _____ involves one desk shared between several people who use the desk at different times.

   a. 28-hour day
   b. 33 Strategies of War
   c. 1990 Clean Air Act
   d. Hot desking

39. _____ is a method of supporting unassigned seating in an office environment. It is similar and is sometimes confused with hot desking, another method of supporting unassigned seating. _____ is reservation-based unassigned seating, whereas, hot desking is reservation-less unassigned seating.

   a. 1990 Clean Air Act
   b. Hotelling
   c. 33 Strategies of War
   d. 28-hour day

40. A _____ is a form of periodic payment from an employer to an employee, which may be specified in an employment contract. It is contrasted with piece wages, where each job, hour or other unit is paid separately, rather than on a periodic basis.

   From the point of a view of running a business, _____ can also be viewed as the cost of acquiring human resources for running operations, and is then termed personnel expense or _____ expense.

   a. Human resource management
   b. Salary
   c. Human resources
   d. Training and development

41. A _____ is a compensation, usually financial, received by a worker in exchange for their labor.

Chapter 16. Building a New Venture Team and Planning for the Next Generation

Compensation in terms of _____s is given to worker and compensation in terms of salary is given to employees. Compensation is a monetary benefits given to employees in returns of the services provided by them.

a. Wage
b. Performance-related pay
c. Profit-sharing agreement
d. State Compensation Insurance Fund

42. In finance, an _____ is a contract between a buyer and a seller that gives the buyer the right--but not the obligation-- to buy or to sell a particular asset (the underlying asset) at a later day at an agreed price. In return for granting the _____, the seller collects a payment (the premium) from the buyer. A call _____ gives the buyer the right to buy the underlying asset; a put _____ gives the buyer of the _____ the right to sell the underlying asset.

a. AAAI
b. Option
c. A Stake in the Outcome
d. A4e

43. In economics and sociology, an _____ is any factor (financial or non-financial) that enables or motivates a particular course of action, or counts as a reason for preferring one choice to the alternatives. It is an expectation that encourages people to behave in a certain way. Since human beings are purposeful creatures, the study of _____ structures is central to the study of all economic activity (both in terms of individual decision-making and in terms of co-operation and competition within a larger institutional structure.)

a. AAAI
b. A4e
c. A Stake in the Outcome
d. Incentive

44. The _____ or gross domestic income (GDI), a basic measure of an economy's economic performance, is the market value of all final goods and services made within the borders of a nation in a year. _____ can be defined in three ways, all of which are conceptually identical. First, it is equal to the total expenditures for all final goods and services produced within the country in a stipulated period of time (usually a 365-day year).

a. Human capital
b. Productivity management
c. Perfect competition
d. Gross domestic product

45. _____ involves having senior executives periodically review their top executives and those in the next lower level to determine several backups for each senior position. This is important because it often takes years of grooming to develop effective senior managers. There is a critical shortage in companies of middle and top leaders for the next five years.

a. Risk management
b. Kanban
c. Trademark
d. Succession planning

46. A _____ may be thought of as a sort of 'premarital agreement' between business partners/shareholders. It is sometimes called a 'business will'. An insured _____ is often recommended by business succession specialists and financial planners to ensure the buy-sell arrangement is well-funded and also to guarantee there will be money when the buy-sell event is triggered.

a. Trade credit
b. 1990 Clean Air Act
c. Buy-sell agreement
d. Countertrade

47. _____ is the process of disposing of an estate. _____ typically attempts to eliminate uncertainties over the administration of a probate and maximize the value of the estate by reducing taxes and other expenses. Guardians are often designated for minor children and beneficiaries in incapacity.

Chapter 16. Building a New Venture Team and Planning for the Next Generation

a. A4e
b. A Stake in the Outcome
c. AAAI
d. Estate planning

48. A _____ is typically created as part of an A/B Living trust estate plan after the death of the first spouse to die. During life, a married couple transfers ownership of property into a trust. Upon the death of the first party to die, the terms of the trust require that some portion of the property be transferred into 'TRUST A' and some other portion into 'TRUST B.' The first of these trusts, A, holds property that remains accessible to the surviving spouse during his or her life.

a. Bypass trust
b. 1990 Clean Air Act
c. 28-hour day
d. Joint and several liability

49. In business and accounting, _____s are everything of value that is owned by a person or company. Any property or object of value that one possesses, usually considered as applicable to the payment of one's debts is considered an _____. Simplistically stated, _____s are things of value that can be readily converted into cash.

a. A Stake in the Outcome
b. Asset
c. AAAI
d. A4e

50. A _____ is a form of partnership similar to a general partnership, except that in addition to one or more general partners (GPs), there are one or more limited partners (_____s.) It is a partnership in which only one partner is required to be a general partner.

The GPs are, in all major respects, in the same legal position as partners in a conventional firm, i.e. they have management control, share the right to use partnership property, share the profits of the firm in predefined proportions, and have joint and several liability for the debts of the partnership.

a. Pension fund
b. Private equity
c. Growth capital
d. Limited partnership

51. A _____ is a type of business entity in which partners (owners) share with each other the profits or losses of the business. _____s are often favored over corporations for taxation purposes, as the _____ structure does not generally incur a tax on profits before it is distributed to the partners (i.e. there is no dividend tax levied.) However, depending on the _____ structure and the jurisdiction in which it operates, owners of a _____ may be exposed to greater personal liability than they would as shareholders of a corporation.

a. Federal Employers Liability Act
b. Mediation
c. Due process
d. Partnership

52. A _____ occurs when a financial sponsor acquires a controlling interest in a company's equity and where a significant percentage of the purchase price is financed through leverage (borrowing.) The assets of the acquired company are used as collateral for the borrowed capital, sometimes with assets of the acquiring company. The bonds or other paper issued for _____s are commonly considered not to be investment grade because of the significant risks involved.

a. Growth capital
b. Venture capital
c. Limited partners
d. Leveraged buyout

53. A _____ is an investment transaction by which an entire company or a controlling part of the stock of a company is sold. A firm 'buys out' a company to take control of it. A _____ can take the form of a leveraged _____, a venture capital _____ or a management _____.

a. Sweat equity
b. Gross profit
c. Shareholder value
d. Buyout

ANSWER KEY

Chapter 1
1. a	2. d	3. c	4. b	5. d	6. a	7. c	8. d	9. c	10. b
11. b	12. d	13. d	14. d	15. c	16. a	17. d	18. c	19. b	20. d
21. c	22. d	23. d	24. d	25. d	26. d	27. c	28. d	29. d	30. c
31. b	32. b	33. c	34. b	35. d	36. b	37. c	38. b		

Chapter 2
1. d	2. b	3. d	4. d	5. c	6. d	7. d	8. b	9. a	10. c
11. d	12. a	13. a	14. d	15. d	16. c	17. d	18. c	19. b	20. d
21. d	22. d	23. a	24. c						

Chapter 3
1. b	2. a	3. d	4. d	5. d	6. d	7. c	8. b	9. d	10. b
11. d	12. b	13. c	14. d	15. c	16. d	17. d	18. a	19. d	20. d
21. c	22. d	23. d	24. d	25. d	26. d				

Chapter 4
1. d	2. a	3. d	4. d	5. d	6. d	7. d	8. c	9. d	10. d
11. b	12. a	13. d	14. b	15. d	16. d	17. c	18. d	19. d	20. d
21. d	22. a	23. c	24. c	25. d	26. a	27. a	28. d	29. d	30. b
31. d									

Chapter 5
1. c	2. a	3. a	4. a	5. b	6. a	7. b	8. a	9. c	10. d
11. d	12. b	13. d	14. b	15. a	16. d	17. d	18. d	19. d	20. d
21. a	22. c	23. c	24. d	25. d	26. d	27. b	28. d	29. b	30. b

Chapter 6
1. c	2. d	3. c	4. d	5. c	6. d	7. a	8. c	9. a	10. d
11. c	12. c	13. c	14. d	15. d	16. d	17. b	18. b	19. d	20. d
21. a	22. c	23. c	24. d	25. d	26. c	27. a	28. d	29. d	30. d
31. d									

Chapter 7
1. d	2. d	3. d	4. d	5. d	6. a	7. d	8. a	9. a	10. d
11. d	12. b	13. d	14. d	15. b	16. d	17. d	18. a	19. d	20. b
21. c	22. d	23. d	24. a	25. d	26. d	27. d	28. d	29. d	30. d
31. b	32. a	33. c	34. c	35. c	36. d	37. d	38. c	39. a	40. d
41. d	42. b	43. d	44. a	45. b	46. c	47. d			

Chapter 8
1. b	2. d	3. d	4. a	5. d	6. d	7. d	8. b	9. b	10. b
11. d	12. a	13. d	14. d	15. d	16. a	17. d	18. a	19. c	20. d
21. b	22. b	23. b	24. a	25. d	26. c	27. d	28. b	29. d	30. a
31. d	32. d	33. a	34. d	35. d	36. b	37. b	38. d	39. d	40. c
41. d	42. d	43. b							

Chapter 9
1. d	2. c	3. d	4. d	5. d	6. d	7. a	8. a	9. c	10. d
11. c	12. a	13. b	14. c	15. d	16. d	17. d	18. d	19. b	20. d
21. d	22. a	23. b	24. c	25. d	26. c	27. b	28. d	29. b	30. d
31. b	32. d	33. c	34. d	35. d	36. d	37. c			

Chapter 10
1. d	2. d	3. a	4. d	5. a	6. c	7. b	8. d	9. b	10. a
11. d	12. d	13. c	14. c	15. a	16. b	17. b	18. b	19. d	20. d

Chapter 11
1. b	2. a	3. d	4. c	5. b	6. a	7. c	8. a	9. c	10. b
11. d	12. d	13. d	14. a	15. d	16. d	17. d	18. b	19. d	20. d
21. b	22. d	23. d	24. c	25. d	26. d	27. d	28. c	29. d	30. d
31. d	32. d	33. d	34. a	35. d	36. d	37. b	38. a		

Chapter 12
1. a	2. d	3. d	4. b	5. a	6. c	7. d	8. b	9. d	10. a
11. a	12. c	13. a	14. d	15. d	16. d	17. d	18. a	19. b	20. d
21. c	22. d	23. d	24. c	25. d					

Chapter 13
1. b	2. a	3. d	4. c	5. d	6. a	7. d	8. d	9. d	10. b
11. a	12. d	13. a	14. b	15. a	16. d	17. d	18. b	19. c	20. d
21. b	22. c	23. d	24. a	25. a	26. a	27. d	28. d	29. d	30. d
31. b	32. b	33. d	34. d	35. d	36. d	37. d	38. d	39. c	

Chapter 14
1. b	2. b	3. d	4. b	5. b	6. a	7. d	8. d	9. d	10. c
11. d	12. d	13. b	14. d	15. b	16. b	17. d	18. d	19. d	20. d
21. d	22. a	23. d	24. b	25. c	26. d	27. d	28. c	29. d	

Chapter 15
1. a	2. b	3. d	4. a	5. b	6. c	7. d	8. d	9. c	10. c
11. d	12. d	13. d	14. d	15. c	16. d	17. c	18. a	19. d	20. d
21. a	22. d	23. b	24. d	25. d	26. b	27. d	28. d	29. b	30. d
31. d	32. a	33. b	34. d						

ANSWER KEY

Chapter 16

1. b	2. d	3. d	4. b	5. d	6. a	7. d	8. d	9. a	10. a
11. d	12. b	13. c	14. c	15. d	16. d	17. d	18. d	19. d	20. d
21. d	22. d	23. d	24. b	25. a	26. b	27. d	28. d	29. d	30. b
31. d	32. d	33. a	34. a	35. d	36. a	37. a	38. d	39. b	40. b
41. a	42. b	43. d	44. d	45. d	46. c	47. d	48. a	49. b	50. d
51. d	52. d	53. d							

www.ingramcontent.com/pod-product-compliance
Lightning Source LLC
Chambersburg PA
CBHW082044230426
43670CB00016B/2774